Voluntary Student Clubs

An Area For Adding Value And Gaining Competitive Advantage

James Daughtry

Abidan
Fox Lake, IL

Copyright © 2011 James Daughtry

All rights reserved.

Published by Abidan

Fox Lake, IL 60020

Abidan@mail.com

ISBN-13: 978-0-615-44372-0

ISBN: 0-615-44372-9

LCCN: 2011901474

This thesis is dedicated to my father
who passed away while I was in Mexico.

Acknowledgements

I would like to thank the following:

my family,

my friends in the United States,

my church family in the United States,

my host families in Mexico,

my friends in Mexico,

my professors at the University of the Americas, especially Dr. Raúl Valdez and Dr. Mark Ryan for their assistance with this thesis.

"Now unto the King eternal, immortal, invisible, the only wise God, be honour and glory for ever and ever. Amen."
                       1 Timothy 1:17

Responsibility for Content

The opinions and ideas expressed in this thesis are not those of the University of the Americas or the Department of Business Administration and should be attributed exclusively to the author.

Table of Contents

Index of Tables xi
Index of Figures xiii

Chapter 1 Introduction 1
    1.1 Hypothesis 1
    1.2 General Objectives 2
    1.3 Specific Objectives 2
    1.4 Scope 2
    1.5 Limitations 3
    1.6 Justification 3
    1.7 Mexican Higher Education 4
    1.8 The University of the Americas 5
    1.9 Methodology 6

Chapter 2 Theoretical Framework 9
    2.1 Concepts and Terminology 9
    2.2 History of Voluntary Student Clubs 10
    2.3 Competitive Analysis of Mexican Universities 14
    2.4 Benchmarking: Learning From The Best 15
    2.5 Literary Review 18

Chapter 3 Methodology 27
    3.1 Hypothesis 27
    3.2 Constructs 28
    3.3 Measuring Instrument 30
    3.4 The Sample 31
    3.5 Pilot Test 32
    3.6 Internal Consistency Reliability 33
    3.7 Official Test 34

Chapter 4 Analysis 35
    4.1 Scale Weight Values 35
    4.2 Pilot Test 36
    4.3 Official Test 38
    4.4 Interpretation 43
    4.5 Confidence Levels 51

Chapter 5 Conclusions **53**
    5.1 Summery of Research 53
    5.2 The Phenomenon of Voluntary Student Clubs 54
    5.3 Further Research 56

Chapter 6 Recommendations **61**
    6.1 Recognition of Voluntary Student Clubs 61
    6.2 Criteria for Voluntary Student Clubs 62
    6.3 Privileges of Voluntary Student Clubs 64
    6.4 Christian Religious Clubs 64
    6.5 Religious Student Clubs and the Mexican Constitution 66

Epilogue **69**

Bibliography **71**

Appendix A: Sample Questionnaire **77**
Appendix B: Pilot Test Questionnaire Data **81**
Appendix C: Reliability Analysis **83**
Appendix D: Pilot Test Weighted Data **89**
Appendix E: Official Test Participant Data **91**
Appendix F: Official Test Weighted Data **93**

Notes **95**

Index of Tables

Table 2.0 Initial Benchmarking Research 16

Table 4.1 Pilot Test Results 36

Table 4.2 Pilot Test Item Scores 37

Table 4.3 Pilot Test Construct Scores 38

Table 4.4 Official Test Participant Data Summary 39

Table 4.5 Official Test Total Responses 41

Table 4.6 Official Test Results 44

Table 4.7 Official Test Item Scores 45

Table 4.8 Official Test Construct Scores 45

Index of Figures

Figure 4.1 Official Test Participant Categories 39

Figure 4.2 Official Test University Experience 40

Figure 4.3 Official Test Education Experience 41

Figure 4.4 Official Test Total Responses 42

Chapter 1

Introduction

This chapter provides an overview of the thesis. The chapter includes the hypothesis, the general and specific objectives, the scope, limitations, justification, a brief overview of Mexican higher education, the presentation of the University of the Americas, and an outline of the methodology.

1.1 Hypothesis

As globalization increases competition, companies are being forced to analyze and improve their products and services to add value and gain a competitive advantage. In an effort to improve as an institution, the University of the Americas constantly evaluates the services that it offers. One area where the University may be able to improve its service, add value and gain a competitive advantage is in the area of voluntary student clubs. This area has been virtually unexplored by the University.

In contrast, universities in the United States have well-developed policies that allow voluntary student clubs to flourish. At U.S. universities, voluntary student clubs often exist in phenomenal numbers. This thesis investigates the area of voluntary student clubs at seven of the top universities in the United States from the standpoint of business administration. The hypothesis of the thesis is that the University of the Americas could add value and gain a competitive advantage at a national and international level through voluntary student clubs that possess official status in the University.

1.2 General Objective

The general objective of the thesis is to examine voluntary student clubs as an area where the University of the Americas could add value and gain a competitive advantage.

1.3 Specific Objectives

The specific objectives of the thesis are:

- To compare the University of the Americas with the top universities in the United States in the area of voluntary student clubs.
- To analyze the top Mexican universities in the area of voluntary student clubs.
- To provide recommendations concerning a voluntary student club system.
- To provide recommendations concerning voluntary student Christian religious clubs.

1.4 Scope

Although the primary focus of the thesis involves the area of marketing, the thesis encompasses many different areas in the field of business administration, including organizational structure, human resource management, information technology, and accounting. In addition, the thesis involves other fields, including education, sociology and religion.

While the findings of the research for this thesis may be useful for other applications, the purpose of the research is to analyze voluntary student clubs as a possible area where the University of the Americas could add value and gain a competitive advantage. The thesis includes recommendations for the development of policy and guidelines for the administration of such clubs based on the existing models at the benchmark universities.

The thesis has a special focus on Christian religious clubs for two main reasons. First, in a preliminary review of approximately 100 U.S. university websites, including the seven benchmark universities, the author found that officially recognized Christian religious clubs existed on all of the campuses. In most cases, a wide variety of these types of clubs were present at the universities. Second, the University of the Americas, by contrast, maintains a strict policy that prohibits religious activity or expression on campus. The University bases this policy on the fact that it was established with a philosophy of being independent of any religious affiliation. As a result, Christian religious clubs are strictly prohibited (Dr. Enrique Cardenas, Rector, personal interview January 11, 1999). If the University of the Americas decides to begin a voluntary student club system, it may need to reevaluate this policy regarding religion.

1.5 Limitations

Although this thesis incorporates different areas of business administration, including organizational structure, human resource management, information technology, and accounting, the thesis is not meant to be an exhaustive investigation of these areas. Similarly, the thesis includes other fields such as education, sociology and religion; however, it will not attempt to perform an in-depth investigation into these fields.

The thesis focuses specifically on the positive effects of voluntary student clubs at U.S. universities. The thesis does not attempt to investigate any negative effects related to voluntary student clubs. In Chapter 5: "Conclusions", the possible negative effects of voluntary student clubs and other topics are suggested as areas for further investigation.

Since the Mexican market is relatively unfamiliar with voluntary students clubs, the thesis seeks to justify them as an area where the University of the Americas could add value and gain a competitive advantage by focusing primarily on the practices of the top universities in the United States. While the thesis attempts to provide sufficient evidence to validate the hypothesis, it will not be able to confirm that the results achieved at U.S. universities will be the same at the University of the Americas. In order to determine the implications of voluntary student clubs at the University of the Americas, a real life study would need to be performed, probably over a number of years in which voluntary student clubs actually exist on campus.

1.6 Justification

A growing number of universities are using benchmarking to evaluate and improve their institutions (Epper 1999). The term "benchmark" was used by land surveyors to refer to a mark made on a rock, a wall, or a building which served as a reference point in determining one's current position or altitude. The term originally was a point from which measurements could be made or a standard against which others could be measured (Bogan and English 1994).

The Xerox Corporation is usually credited as being the first to use the term "benchmarking" in the field of business. In 1982, during a corporate training and organizational meeting, Xerox applied this term to a process they employed to identify the performance gap that existed with their competition. The process involved specific standards of measurement in areas such as production costs, cycle time, overhead costs, retail selling prices, and product features compared to those of their chief competitors. One of the main purposes of these comparisons was to identify areas of weakness within Xerox and emulate the best practices of top companies (Spendolini 1992).

According to Bogan and English (1994):

Benchmarking...is simply the systematic process of searching for the best practices, innovative ideas, and highly effective operating procedures that lead to superior performance....By systematically studying the best business practices, operating tactics, and winning strategies of others, an individual, team or organization can accelerate its own progress and improvement.

Similarly, Spendolini (1992) defines benchmarking as a continuous, systematic process for evaluating the products, services, and work processes of organizations that are recognized as representing the best practices for the purpose of organization improvement.

In other words, if a company or university wants to become better or be the best, it needs to compare itself to the best. In the past, it was common for companies to compare themselves to a wide range of companies - the best as well as the worst. This type of approach, however, has several problems. First, it can lead to apathy because companies that rank somewhere in the middle or at the top may feel satisfied knowing there are companies that are worse. Second, if a company is striving to improve, it probably does not need to compare itself to bad companies. Although some lessons may be learned from the mistakes of bad companies, learning from the best companies is a superior method.

In recent years, business administration writers and companies have expanded the concept of benchmarking and developed many specialized theories and models for different areas, situations and industries. This thesis applies the general benchmarking concept of comparing yourself to the best in order to learn and become like the best or surpass them. "At the most fundamental level, benchmarking means learning from others. The skill is honed into an art by identifying and then comparing your own company to others who are very strong at what they do" (Bogan and English 1994).

As the University of the Americas seeks to improve as an institution, it must compare itself with the best universities of the world in all areas. This thesis will focus on one of these areas: voluntary student clubs. Currently, the University of the Americas does not have a voluntary student club system. All of the benchmark universities in the United States have well-established ones. Since U.S. universities are recognized as being among the best in the world, all of the areas that contribute to the success of these universities should be evaluated and considered.

1.7 Mexican Higher Education

The National Autonomous University of Mexico City (UNAM) has been the main center of higher education since 1551, when it was founded as the University of Mexico. The University was originally designed to serve the political purposes of the Spanish colonial regime, particularly by developing religious philosophy to fight protestant theology. During the struggle for Mexican independence, the University closed and reopened several times. In 1929, after a student movement, the University was granted autonomy (Currie and Newson 1998; Brock and Clarkson 1990).

The dominant institutional image for higher education in Mexico has been public universities, with the UNAM being the prototype and most influential model. Although most of the public universities are relatively independent, they have primarily followed the UNAM in educational practice. The programs have traditionally focused on the sociopolitical agenda of providing increased employment opportunities to further Mexico's economic development. As a result, the curriculum was designed primarily to train students for a particular profession.

In recent years, however, the trend in higher education has been shifting toward more diversification and liberal arts studies. This trend is a result of the opening of the Mexican economy through the privatization of state owned companies, the loosening of restrictions to foreign investment, and the North American Free Trade Agreement. As Mexico is being thrust into the global economy, Mexican universities are responding with new curriculum to meet these challenges.

Another significant development in Mexican higher education has been the emergence of private universities. Since the 1980's, the upper and middle class increasingly have been sending their children to private institutions. A number of these private universities have gained prestige by using a liberal arts model of education (Kent 1998; Botzman and Kim 1997).

1.8 The University of the Americas

In 1940, Dr. Henry Cain and Dr. Paul Murray founded the University of the Americas in Mexico City as Mexico City College. At the time, Dr. Cain was superintendent of the American elementary school and Dr. Murray was director of the American high school. Dr. Cain served as the first rector of the College. At the first graduation ceremony in 1944, a total of 20 students received associate degrees.

Since the founding of the College, the University of the Americas has been influenced by American values and philosophy, and has had strong ties with the United States. In 1951, the College was accepted as a member of the Texas College Association. By 1959, the Southern Association of Colleges and Schools granted the College American accreditation.

In 1963, the College changed its name to University of the Americas. Four years later, the Mary Street Jenkins Foundation donated the American Elementary School in Puebla to the University. With funding from the International Development Agency, the University was established at this new location.

In 1968, the University changed its name to the Spanish equivalent, "Universidad de las Américas." The same year, the state of Puebla officially recognized their educational programs. During this time, the University also began construction of the new campus in San Andres Cholula, and by 1970 it had relocated to the new site.

In 1975, the University named Dr. Fernando Macías Rendón the first Mexican Rector. Dr. Macías greatly increased the enrollment of Mexican students at the University. Until that time, the majority of the students had been American.

Currently, the Universidad de las Américas is one of the most prestigious universities in Mexico. It offers 36 bachelors degrees, 24 masters degrees, and two doctorates. While the majority of the students are Mexican, the University attracts scholars from the United States, Latin America, and Europe as well as many other parts of the world (Universidad de las Américas 2001).

1.9 Methodology

The Theoretical Framework of the thesis utilizes the following:

<u>Competitive Benchmarking</u>

- Examination of voluntary student clubs at the best universities in the United States.
- Benchmarking analysis of voluntary student clubs at the University of the Americas.

<u>Competitive Analysis</u>

- Examination of voluntary student clubs at the best Mexican universities.
- Benchmarking analysis of voluntary student clubs at the University of the Americas.

<u>Literary Review</u>

- Review of university websites, books, magazines, and other publications.
- Selection of relevant information
- Interpretation of information

The Methodology Chapter utilizes a quantitative-descriptive approach. The empirical evidence was obtained by research questionnaires directed to college administrators and faculty at the benchmark universities. The methodology includes the following:

- Determination of variables
- Development of instrument
- Selection of pilot sample

- Data collection
- Processing of data
- Internal consistency reliability analysis of instrument
- Selection of official sample
- Data collection
- Processing of data

The Analysis Chapter utilizes the following:

- Charts and tables
- Comments of respondents
- Evaluation of data
- Interpretation of data

Chapter 2

Theoretical Framework

In this chapter, important terms and concepts used in this thesis are defined. The chapter also provides a history of voluntary student clubs, presents initial benchmarking research, and furnishes a summary of the author's literary review.

2.1 Concepts and Terminology

Since the focus of this thesis is on voluntary student clubs, it is important to clarify the meaning of this phrase. Universities throughout the United States have many extracurricular activities, including sports teams, student government, and university clubs, which are organized and directed by the university. Voluntary students clubs differ in many ways from these types of activities. One of the main differences is that voluntary student clubs are initiated and directed by students and not the university. Another important difference is that all students have the opportunity to participate in voluntary student clubs, whereas sports teams, student government and some university clubs are limited to individuals who are able to fulfill the necessary requirements.

Voluntary student clubs also differ from fraternities. In general, voluntary student groups are established with a specific purpose or orientation such as academic, artistic, ethnic, political, environmental, public service and religious. Although in some cases membership maybe limited to students who meet the criteria of the club, the meetings and activities are usually open to the entire university. Fraternities, on the other hand, often do not have a specific purpose, but rather encompass many different areas of student life, including housing, meals and social activities. The meetings and activities are usually open only to members of the fraternity.

After a preliminary review of approximately 100 U.S. university websites, the author found that most U.S. universities have well-established policies to encourage and foster the development of voluntary student clubs. Upon registration and acceptance, the clubs usually receive status as officially recognized student organizations of the university and are granted privileges such as the use of university facilities and the university name, and in many cases are provided financial assistance.

Most of these college campuses host many different religious clubs; the most common are usually Christian religious clubs. As mentioned in the introduction, while considering the overall impact of voluntary student clubs, this thesis will specifically examine Christian religious clubs. The phrase "Christian religious clubs" will refer in general to all Catholic, Protestant, Orthodox and Interdenominational Christian clubs.

Two other important phrases frequently used in business administration and throughout this thesis are "adding value" and "competitive advantage." These two phrases are closely related. According to Michael Porter (1985), "competitive advantage grows fundamentally out of the value a firm is able to create for its buyers."

As the phrase implies, "adding value" involves giving worth or increasing the worth of a product or service. "A firm creates value for its buyer…if it lowers its buyer's cost or raises the buyer's performance in ways the buyer cannot match by purchasing from competitors." The ultimate worth or "ultimate value a firm creates is measured by the amount buyers are willing to pay for its product or service" (Porter 1990).

The phrase "competitive advantage" involves gaining some type of a benefit over rival companies. A competitive advantage is achieved through a firm's value chain. The value chain refers to "many discrete activities a firm performs in designing, producing, marketing, delivering, and supporting its product." Simply stated, "A firm gains competitive advantage by performing these strategically important activities more cheaply or better than its competitors" (Porter 1985).

2.2 History of Voluntary Student Clubs

The history of student associations began in the twelfth century with the very origins of universities. As students and teachers first gathered in urban centers in Italy, students organized associations for protection. Actually, the word "university" means "totality of a group" and was first used to describe these student associations (Horowitz 1987).

In colonial New England, Christian students founded the first college club at Harvard College in 1719. These pious students met together "for the worship of God." From this simple beginning, Christian religious clubs have spread throughout the country. Today, Christian religious clubs exists on virtually every college campus in the United States (Morison 1964).

In 1728, literary societies appeared at Harvard, and a more lasting society began meeting at Yale in 1753. The literary society movement eventually spread to almost every U.S. college. Students usually formed two societies on campus and engaged in debates. Since the formal classroom instruction of the universities was dry, dominated by reciting and testing of memorized texts, these societies provided the students with an opportunity for personal growth. Although college authorities were generally hostile toward self-expression or interpretation in the classroom, they approved of the literary societies and generally provided space for their activities. The literary societies provided an arena for the development of "character, leadership, imagination, self-reliance – and therefore were surely construed by the college authorities as fulfilling in action what the senior course in moral philosophy could provide only in theory and guidance" (Rudolph 1977).

The literary societies came to hold a dominant place in campus life and provided an excellent source of education for public life. Although the themes they studied were outside of the formal university curriculum, the two were complementary (Horowitz 1987).

With respect to his undergraduate experience at Yale, a board member of Yale in 1828 stated, "No part of my training at Yale College seems to me to have been more beneficial than that which I derived from the practice of speaking and debating in the literary society to which I belonged." Similarly, a Princeton alumnus in regard to his literary society declared, "It was worth more as a part of education than the college itself, not only in a literary point of view, but in manners and morals" (Rudolph 1977).

By the 1820's, literary societies started to decline and a different student movement began - fraternities. The fraternities were very different from the literary societies. Unlike the literary societies of the eighteenth century, the fraternities consisted of a small, select group pledged to secrecy. The main concern of fraternities "was to create within the larger college a small group of compatible fellows for friendship, mutual protection, and good times." By 1840, most of New England colleges had fraternities, and the movement was established in the Midwest prior to 1850 (Horowitz 1987).

Since many of the early fraternities excluded students and were often in conflict with the university, other students began to form anti-secret fraternities. The anti-secrecy fraternities movement also spread to colleges throughout the country. In 1847, students groups from several universities met and formed the Anti-Secret Confederation that later became Delta Upsilon, a national anti-secrecy fraternity that still exists today (Horowitz 1987; Delta Upsilon 2002).

As the fraternities were growing, the literary societies were decreasing and by 1870 had virtually disappeared. Several reasons are cited for their decline. First, the literary societies declined not specifically because the fraternities defeated their purpose, but because the fraternities created a higher level of loyalty and created political complications in the society elections. Second, literary societies declined as the colleges themselves began to open the libraries more than once a week, build up broader collections of books, introduce respectable study in English literature, explore history as a field of study, and expand the study of sciences (Rudolph 1962).

In addition to fraternities, during this time period various student clubs sprang up on college campuses. These clubs grew as they eagerly welcomed new students into their membership. By the early 1900's, almost every college campus was the scene of vigorous activity by numerous student clubs. These extracurricular student clubs tended to be of two main types. The first type was clubs concerned with a special academic field, such as history or English, in which faculty members participated along with students. The second type was clubs directed by the students alone. The student directed clubs catered to every conceivable interest, "There were, for example, religious clubs, music clubs, drama clubs, glee clubs, debating clubs, mandolin clubs, hobby clubs, and many other clubs" (Brubaker and Rudy 1976).

After the Civil War was when college life truly began to develop and extracurricular student activities became an important part of the college experience. As successful alumni began to donate large sums of money to support extracurricular activities, universities began realizing the importance of such activities. The official position of universities changed to support of these activities, resulting in better relations between administration and the students. "In the early twentieth century as presidents and deans empowered college men as official student leaders, the canon of college life shifted from antagonism to support of the administration" (Horowitz 1987).

As colleges began to support extracurricular student clubs, they created new positions that enlisted faculty members to supervise the student activities. By 1930, a college administration textbook maintained that colleges with an enrollment of over 300 students should have a dean to supervise, advise, and inspire the non-academic life of the students. The responsibilities of the dean included working with student leaders to help plan and coordinate student activities and make them compatible with the administration's goals. "As deans of men and women cooperated with the leaders of student society in planning events and enforcing codes of conduct, the apparent distinctions between institutional goals and those of college life faded" (Horowitz 1987).

During the 1960's, a wide variety of new clubs began to emerge on campuses. Unlike the large clubs of previous generations, these clubs were relatively small, probably due in part to the greater number of clubs competing for members. Hobby and personal interest clubs became especially common. Major and career clubs also gained popularity. Political, peace and antiwar groups were popular on college campuses while the Vietnam conflict raged, but the clubs they spawned greatly declined after the U.S withdrawal from Southeast Asia. Religious clubs also increased in number, especially Christian religious clubs (Levine 1980).

While Christian religious clubs have a long history on college campuses, they have grown and become better established in recent years (Tucker 1983). Although many reasons may exist for their increase, one of the main reasons may be the result of the Equal Access Act that removed the barriers for religious clubs that existed at many universities:

The Act was passed by the Congress in 1984 to end the widespread discrimination against student religious groups that was occurring in many public secondary schools... Both the Congress and the Supreme Court have made it clear that equal access for secondary students' religious speech is the legally correct course that school administrators must follow. Discrimination against students' religious speech is censorship and is impermissible under the Equal Access Act and the First Amendment...It mandates that any public secondary school which allows one or more noncurriculum related student groups to meet must allow students to meet for religious, political, philosophical or other speech (Colby 1993).

Data from the 1990's shows that the trend continues toward smaller and more specialized clubs. Support and advocacy clubs largely have taken the place of political groups. These clubs "have often acted as advocates, identifying problems the members faced, educating both members and the larger community about those problems, and seeking remedies." The modern roots of these types of clubs go back to the 1960's with the rise of black student associations. As gender became an important issue in the 1970's, women's groups became popular. During the 1980's and 1990's, the focus of clubs has been on race, ethnicity, sexual orientation and disabilities. Latino clubs are among the most commonly appearing new clubs on campus. While International clubs are growing, they also are becoming specialized. International students are forming clubs according to countries, regions of a country, dialects, etc (Levine and Cureton 1998).

Across the United States voluntary student clubs are being formed for "every type of hobby, sport, religion, or ethnic group. Smaller groups are breaking off from larger ones. General-interest groups are becoming specialized. And some groups are simply being duplicated." This division and multiplication of campus clubs is being viewed in two ways. "Many college officials and students see the growth as a positive sign of vibrancy of campus life." Other college officials "worry that the division and multiplication of campus organizations are contributing to the Balkanization and segregation of student life" (Reisberg 2000).

The proliferation of clubs definitely seems to be causing a decline in the number of members per club as well as creating less stability within clubs. The expanding numbers of clubs means that there are more groups with tiny constituencies competing for political influence on campus. The shrinking size of clubs makes it increasingly difficult for them to find effective leaders and to maintain continuity in leadership (Levine and Cureton 1998).

With each new generation, voluntary student clubs experience change. Some clubs, like literary societies, have virtually disappeared. Others, like Christian religious clubs, have endured. While no one can be certain what type of changes will occur and what kind of clubs will exist this century, based on over 280 years of history one thing is almost certain, voluntary student clubs will continue to thrive on U.S college campuses.

2.3 Competitive Analysis of Mexican Universities

This section provides a concise examination of voluntary student clubs at six top Mexican universities that would be considered competitors of the University of the Americas (Laura Leon, recruiter, personal interview, July 18, 2000). The information about these universities was obtained from their web sites. In some cases, the information available was extremely limited. While some of the universities list a number of clubs, most of these clubs did not appear to meet the definition given in this thesis for voluntary student clubs. The clubs were usually organizations or workshops sponsored and directed by the university, such as student government, clubs organized by departments for students in a particular major, recreational programs, and sports clinics. Two universities, however, appeared to have a few clubs that met the criteria of a voluntary student club. None of the websites provided information on starting a club or mentioned a voluntary student club system. The six universities are:

Tecnológico de Monterrey, Monterrey, México
The university lists a number official student clubs, but most of these clubs appear to be organized and directed by the university. Some of the clubs, however, may qualify as voluntary student clubs. An interesting statement is made on the student development web page, "Mucho de lo que necesito saber lo aprendí en grupos estudiantiles" (Much of what I need to know, I learned in student groups).

Universidad Autónoma de Guadalajara, Guadalajara, Jalisco, México
The university lists four clubs, two of which may satisfy the definition of a voluntary student club. They are:

- <u>Sociedad de Estudiantes Latinoamericanos</u> (The Society of Latin American Students). This club promotes unity between students of Central and South America.
- <u>El Instituto de Ingenieros Electricistas y Electrónicos</u> (The Institute of Electrical and Electronic Engineers). This organization is dedicated to the advance of the theory and applications of electrical and electronic engineering. It belongs to the international organization the IEEE, which is the world's largest professional and technical society in this area.

Universidad Iberoamericana Santa Fe, México DF, México
The university lists a few clubs, but does not provide many details. The clubs do not appear to meet the definition of voluntary student clubs.

Universidad Anahuac, México DF, México
The university lists no official voluntary student clubs. The website has an interesting statement, "Al final de nuestras vidas lo único que queda es lo que hayamos hecho por Dios y por nuestros hermanos los hombres" (At the end of our lives the only thing that remains is what we have done for God and for our brothers, mankind) P. Marcial Maciel, L.C.

Universidad De La Salle, México DF, México
The university lists no official voluntary student clubs.

Instituto Tecnológico Autónomo de México, México DF, México
The university lists no official voluntary student clubs.

These Mexican universities appear similar to the University of the Americas with regard to voluntary student clubs. Although some clubs may exist, the universities do not appear to have an established voluntary student club system. Therefore, an opportunity may exist for the University of the Americas to gain a competitive advantage over the competition in the Mexican market by implementing a voluntary student club system.

2.4 Benchmarking: Learning From The Best

While the origin of benchmarking usually is credited to the business world, Epper (1999) contends, "In many ways, and perhaps without realizing it, colleges and universities have always engaged in benchmarking. We have long compared ourselves to our peers while aspiring to greater levels of enrollment, funding, recognition, and prestige."

Although benchmarking can be a valuable tool in higher education, Epper (1999) states, "Colleges and universities do not come to benchmarking easily for many reasons, not the least of which is that it is a humbling experience. It requires us to look deeply at ourselves, to recognize our weaknesses, and to look elsewhere for examples of how to do things better."

For the University of the Americas, as well as for other universities, acknowledging deficiencies may not be easy, however, this could be the simplest step in benchmarking. According to Epper (1999):

> The greatest challenge in benchmarking, of course, is putting the results to good use after the study is completed. After all, the ultimate objective of benchmarking is to generate action: to change, and to improve…In spite of theses challenges, benchmarking has a strong potential to help colleges and universities learn from themselves and others.

In this thesis, the top seven undergraduate universities in the United States according to the 2001 rankings by *US News and World Report* will be the basis for the benchmarking. *US News* provides the principal and most widely disseminated rankings of universities. The rankings are based on several key measures of quality that fall into seven broad categories: academic reputation; retention (freshman retention and six-year graduation rate); faculty resources; student selectivity (for example, average admission test scores of incoming students); financial resources; alumni giving; and, for national universities, an indicator of graduation rate performance. While everyone may not agree with the exact rankings of *US News*, most would agree that these seven universities are among the best in the United States.

The comparisons of the University of the Americas to the benchmark universities are shown in Table 2.0 Initial Benchmarking Research.

TABLE 2.0 INITIAL BENCHMARKING RESEARCH							
Rank No.	University Name	Religious Affiliation	University Club Policy	Club Web Pages	Registered Clubs	Religious Clubs	Christian Religious Clubs
1	Princeton	None	Yes	Yes	100+	Yes	Yes
2	Harvard	None	Yes	Yes	100+	Yes	Yes
2	Yale	None	Yes	Yes	100+	Yes	Yes
4	CalTech	None	Yes	Yes	75+	Yes	Yes
5	MIT	None	Yes	Yes	300+	Yes	Yes
6	Stanford	None	Yes	Yes	200+	Yes	Yes
6	Penn	None	Yes	Yes	100+	Yes	Yes
-	UDLA	None	No	No	0*	No**	No**

Prepared by the author using information from *US News* as well as the university websites and personal interviews at the University of the Americas.
* A few clubs exist that may possibly meet the criteria for voluntary student clubs.
** The University of the Americas strictly prohibits all religious clubs.

Explanations of Categories in Table 2.0

Rank No. – This category lists the top seven universities beginning with the highest as number 1. Since two universities are tied for second place, both share the number 2 position. The third place is skipped as a result of the tie and the next position is fourth and then fifth. Since two universities tied for sixth place both share the number 6 position. As a Mexican university, the University of the Americas is not included in the ranking.

University Name – Because of space considerations, Table 2.0 uses abbreviations for some of the universities. The official names and locations of the universities are:

- Princeton University, Princeton, New Jersey
- Harvard University, Cambridge, Massachusetts
- Yale University, New Haven, Connecticut
- California Institute of Technology, Pasadena, California
- Massachusetts Institute of Technology, Cambridge, Massachusetts
- Stanford University, Stanford, California
- University of Pennsylvania, Philadelphia, Pennsylvania
- University of the Americas, Puebla, Mexico

Religious Affiliation – This category indicates whether the university is officially affiliated with a religion. Although many universities have religious roots, they do not claim affiliation with a particular denomination.

University Club Policy – This category specifies whether the university has an official published policy for clubs that is available to students.

Club Web Pages – This category indicates whether the universities provide the clubs with space on a university server to create club web pages.

Registered Clubs – This category provides the estimated minimum number of officially registered clubs at the university. The exact number of clubs would be difficult to determine because universities web sites are often not up to date in this area and many universities list all student organizations together, some of which might not meet the definition of a voluntary student club. Due to limitations of this thesis, it is not possible to perform an in-depth investigation on every student organization. Therefore, an estimated minimum number of voluntary student clubs is provided. In most cases, this number is probably much higher.

Religious Clubs – This category indicates if the university has officially registered religious clubs.

Christian Religious Clubs - This category indicates if the university has officially registered Christian Religious clubs.

2.5 Literary Review

The information provided in Table 2.0 Initial Benchmarking Research indicates that all of these top universities have well-established club systems and numerous voluntary student clubs. This evidence alone provides strong support for the hypothesis that the University of the Americas could add value and gain a competitive advantage at a national and international level through voluntary student clubs that possess official status in the university. Nevertheless, we will continue to investigate this subject to obtain additional evidence that will either further substantiate the hypothesis or refute it. The following paragraphs provide a summary of the author's research from printed works and university web sites encompassing or related to the subject of voluntary student clubs.

According to Astin (1985), the principal reason for the existence of universities is "to develop the talents of its students-or, as economists would say, to develop the 'human capital' of the nation…." Therefore, the best universities are the ones that maximize the intellectual and personal development of their students. While many theories exist on how to achieve this type of development, most of the research "points in a single direction: the key to an effective learning experience is involvement."

In order to understand the concept of student involvement, it may be helpful to begin with a general definition:

> Student involvement refers to the quantity and quality of the physical and psychological energy that students invest in the college experience. Such involvement takes many forms, such as absorption in academic work, participation in extracurricular activities, and interaction with faculty and other institutional personnel (Astin, 1984).

In the student involvement theory, Astin (1985) states that there are two basic postulates:

> First, the amount of student learning and personal development associated with any educational program is directly proportional to the quality and quantity of student involvement in that program. And second, the effectiveness of any educational policy or practice is directly related to the capacity of that policy or practice to increase involvement.

On the subject of student involvement, Boyer (1987) considers extracurricular activities and voluntary service as key areas that have a positive effect on the college experience. According to Boyer "Self-generated activity adds vitality to the campus" which is important because "the effectiveness of the undergraduate experience relates to the quality of campus life. It is directly linked to the time students spend on campus and to the quality of their involvement in activities."

Boyer (1990) believes, "Many students, perhaps most, experience the academic community in only marginal and monetary ways. The common ground they share with others is the wish to get ahead, the goal of getting a credential, acquiring a degree." On the other hand, he states that students involved in extracurricular activities and clubs were more satisfied and felt better connected. In addition, he comments, "Many faculty and administrators, especially those at large universities, feel that campus subgroups are prerequisites for a healthy community."

Concerning clubs and groups on campus, Stage (1992) believes, "Campus subcultures are important because they provide their members with the means of coping with the difficulties of college life through social support and guidelines for living."

Upcraft (1985) cites various studies that show student activities have an impact on retention rates. The studies found that some of the factors contributing to higher student retention rates include:

- Belonging to student organizations
- Involvement in social activities
- Involvement in cultural activities
- Using campus facilities
- Participation in extracurricular activities

According to Upcraft (1990), campus activities such as voluntary student clubs contribute to both higher retention rates and the personal development of students. He explains, "the reason for the positive relationship between participation in campus activities and retention and personal development is most likely the influence of students on one another." Although student resident halls provide an environment that can improve student retention and facilitate student development, often only a small percentage of the total student body lives on campus. Therefore, Upcraft suggests that student activities are the only way outside of the classroom that universities can effectively impact the entire student body.

Weingartner (1993) believes that an important area of education exists beyond the classroom. According to Weingartner, "A student should learn to write and calculate in college but also make friends who might later further a career. History is important, but so is learning to take part in group activities….The job of college is the whole person."

Similarly, Boyer (1987) stresses that a college education should do more than provide students with knowledge in a specific area:

In the end, the goal of the undergraduate experience is not only to prepare the undergraduates for careers, but to enable them to live lives of dignity and purpose; not only to give knowledge to the student, but to channel knowledge to humane ends. "It is not learning," said Woodrow Wilson, "but the spirit of service that will give college a place in the annals of the nation."

In addition to helping prepare students for life outside the workplace, involvement in voluntary student clubs may also help to prepare students for future employment. The interpersonal skills that students learn and develop through participation in extracurricular activities may be directly transferable to their job. In their research, Pascarella and Terenzini (1991) found that "Alumni are reasonably consistent in reporting that involvement in extracurricular activities, particularly in leadership roles, significantly enhanced interpersonal leadership skills important to job success."

Assessing the college experience from the standpoint of business, Oblinger and Verville (1998) conclude:

> Many strategic and line managers see the undergraduate experience as having a major positive impact on the personal development of graduates. This personal development is considered at least as important as the intellectual benefits of a degree and often more important than the development of a specific knowledge base.

However, Oblinger and Vervilles (1998) state that business leaders feel that some important areas for improvement of college graduates are communication skills, the ability to work in teams and ethics. Studies results have show that although many graduates considered that their degrees were enormously beneficial both in personal and professional terms, a large number considered that the undergraduate experience did not adequately prepare them for the world of work. Nine out of ten graduates suggest that the degree equipped them for getting a job rather than performing in the workplace.

In regard to workplace preparation, Weingartner (1993) maintains that involvement in extracurricular activities provides the opportunity for students to prepare themselves for employment by learning to collaborate with others. In many extracurricular activities, students must work together to accomplish the desired goals. This experience is extremely valuable and difficult to simulate in more formal pedagogic settings. Regardless whether a group collaborates to put on a play or works to further a social cause, the individuals must fit their own initiatives into the broader one of a corporate entity. Therefore, the students face "experiences that resemble the ways of work in our era."

According to Fry (1996), "getting involved in extracurricular activities…can really pay dividends when it comes to courting prospective employers." Fry explains:

> In addition to the initiative you showed in joining, your involvement may demonstrate evidence of your ability to act as a leader, handle responsibility and get along with many different kinds of people in a job setting - all important work-related qualifications.

In regard to volunteer service, Besson (1994) states, "Potential employers look favorably on candidates who are active participants in organizations." She explains that it "shows your willingness to participate in a worthy cause" and "demonstrates that the volunteer group trusts you to follow through with your commitments." Companies need employees who "want to pursue a common mission, are capable and interested in assuming leadership roles, and know how to gain the respect and cooperation of their peers."

In addition to the positive benefits participation in voluntary student clubs may have on individual students, evidence indicates that additional corporate benefits may exist. According to Pascarella and Terenzini (1991):

> As a group, students who frequently participated in extracurricular activities tend to enter college with relatively high educational aspirations. Consequently, they may constitute a peer group within the institution, a culture whose norms tend to accentuate the educational aspirations of participating members.

On most campuses, student organizations flourish and wane with changing student generations and departmental faculties. Although some fluctuations are unavoidable, Weingartner (1993) recommends that universities implement policies that would make flourishing more likely and decrease the probability that the activity level of voluntary clubs will drop below a certain threshold. He stresses that student extracurricular activities add value to the college experience and universities need to support them.

At Princeton University, student participation in the University community is not only encouraged, it is expected from the students. In regard to the rights and responsibilities of students, Princeton (2000) states:

> As constituents of the academic community, students are expected, individually and collectively, to express their views on issues of institutional policy and on matters of general interest to the student body, student views are especially valuable and will always play an essential role in the formulation of policies affecting student interests. These officers of the University are also available to discuss any matters of importance with any student organization. In addition to these important channels of communication it now seems appropriate to provide other means through which students can make useful contributions to decisions that are of special interest and relevance to their academic, cultural, and social life at Princeton....By drawing on the ideas and talents of students to a greater extent, the cultural and intellectual life of the campus outside the classroom can be stimulated and these activities made more responsive to their perceived needs. And ... there is reason to believe that they can make further contributions that will enhance the conditions of individual and social life at Princeton.

In regard to extracurricular activities including voluntary student clubs, Harvard University (2000) states:

> Believing that extracurricular activities provide students with important opportunities for personal development and growth outside the classroom, the College supports a wide variety of pursuits including public service, the arts, and athletics. Through these activities undergraduates meet other men and women of similar interests, discover an outlet for their talents, and make a valuable contribution to Harvard and the community.

In addition, Harvard University (2000) sees student organizations as providing many others benefits:

> Through undergraduate organizations each new Class leaves its special mark on the cultural, social, and intellectual life of the College. In granting official recognition to these activities, the College seeks to fulfill its commitment to free inquiry and to the importance of an education that encompasses the whole person.

According to Yale University (2000), voluntary student clubs and organizations provide opportunities for students outside the classroom:

> Yale recognizes that organizations under the leadership of undergraduates can and do enhance a student's education by providing additional opportunities beyond the curriculum for personal development and growth. Furthermore, the University benefits from the variety of services and activities provided by undergraduate organizations. The University believes that students should be encouraged to participate in organizations that are open to all members of the community and whose activities do not interfere with the policies or programs of the University or with the rights of other members of the community.

The California Institute of Technology (2000) summarizes the contributions of voluntary student clubs with this statement, "The activities these groups sponsor provide yet another way to de-stress, meet people, and generally turn yourself into that well-rounded person we all know we should be."

Stanford University (2000) "recognizes that student organizations enrich the school, cultural and educational experiences of students and the larger University community" and "supports student organizations and student initiated programs." The office of student affairs at Stanford University maintains as one of their core values, "The involvement of students in a variety of communities and activities enhances their intellectual, emotional, and social growth."

The University of Pennsylvania (2000) states that while they are "a school of great academic strength, strength in academics is not the only quality that identifies its students. Penn students are involved in a myriad of activities that span from ethnic organizations to popular campus publications to community service groups." One of the school's departments is dedicated to providing "world-class services that effectively and efficiently foster the integration of students' intellectual, cultural, personal, recreational, social, and leadership experiences at the University of Pennsylvania" (1997). A specific way that the university seeks to promote student involvement is by providing quality facilities and event assistance. The University of Pennsylvania provides "state-of-the-art classrooms, student union and performing arts spaces offering students the most desirable environment in which to study and engage in co-curricular activity" (1999).

At MIT, a Presidential Task Force on Student Life and Learning performed a comprehensive review of the Institute's educational mission and its implementation. The Task Force examined a multitude of historical and current reports, analyzed numerical data, and conducted surveys of students, faculty, and alumni. In addition, the Task Force held internal meetings with a variety of MIT administrators, sponsors, junior faculty, faculty committees, department and school heads, and other undergraduate officers. Members of the Task Force also met and corresponded with hundreds of other groups and individuals inside and outside of MIT including students, student organizations, and staff members. The Task Force included a Student Advisory Committee composed of roughly two dozen graduate and undergraduate members that provided substantial input and feedback (MIT 1998, Sept.).

The Student Advisory Committee (MIT 1998, April) published a final report, entitled "Putting Education First." In their report, the Committee suggested, "MIT lags behind its peer schools in the number of alumni involved in civic affairs, community leadership, and corporate leadership." The report identified problems and made recommendations for a new direction for the university:

> Our primary recommendation is that a new way of educating students for life should be MIT's top priority. In order to achieve this, every part of the MIT experience inside and outside the classroom should enhance its ability to educate students for life in the 21st century. However, what is most needed is a radical change in MIT's culture and values so that the development of the whole student becomes the highest priority across all areas of MIT - faculty governance, curriculum, the research labs, residential units, student activities, community activities, student services, alumni services and even pre-enrollment services.

In the report, the Committee (MIT 1998, April) emphasized the benefits that students receive through student activities, "As we have already stressed, students gain valuable skills from participation in the MIT community. By running their own affairs, students learn interpersonal and management skills by direct practice." However, the report also emphasized the benefits that the university receives. The Committee explained that students play an enormous role in running the MIT community. Students largely manage their living groups, organize and lead student organizations that provide entertainment, network support, and news to MIT, direct arts and theater groups and sponsor events attended by the entire community, manage volunteer and charity programs that interface with the Cambridge and Boston neighbors, oversee the primary programs that introduce new MIT students to the community, and help organize and supervise as well as participate in athletic activities and events. While the Institute provides some of these activities with funds and programming support, most remain essentially independent.

One of the problems that Student Advisory Committee (MIT 1998, April) identified at MIT was the lack of support and recognition of student leaders and student groups by the Institute. Although students play an important role at the Institute, student leaders receive little or no recognition for their efforts as leaders, and faculty members are typically unaware of which students are leaders. Similarly, although many student organizations are exceedingly well run, frequently on tight budgets and sometimes operated out of dorm rooms, the Institute often overlooks these accomplishments.

The Student Advisory Committee (MIT 1998, April) emphasized the need for improvement in the area of leadership development. Of all the parts of the education for life, they felt MIT was most deficient in teaching leadership skills. The report recommended increased interaction of faculty with student leaders and a community governance system that places value on student participation.

In addition to promoting student development, student activities may also be important for attracting students to the Institute. The report declared that large numbers of the best students were deciding not to apply to MIT. Since MIT's reputation is derived mainly from its research, students feel this could limit their career options. Increasingly, incoming students are becoming more interested in the type of education that will effectively prepare them for life.

Another specific area the Student Advisory Committee (MIT 1998, April) addressed was ethical values. The report advocated that MIT should promote the discussion and formulation of ethical values among their students. The Committee suggested that the Institute use either traditional or nontraditional methods. Since this report focuses on student involvement, student organizations may play a part in addressing this topic. Often student organizations are involved with ethical issues and host forums for discussion.

According to the Presidential Task Force on Student Life and Learning (MIT 1998, Sept.), the central finding was that the interaction among student life and learning in the student's experience is fundamental. The Task Force states:

> The combination of structured learning and unstructured or informal education is critical because it enables us to educate the whole student. It is this very combination that results in MIT's reputation for providing a world-class education, as opposed to a merely skill-based or knowledge-based education.

However, the Task Force (MIT 1998, Sept.) admits that while the combination of formal learning and informal learning already takes place at MIT, "the relationship between them is sometimes undervalued in the way the Institute thinks about education." It acknowledges that in many ways, informal learning plays a bigger role in defining an MIT education than the formal curriculum does, and therefore MIT must have an appropriate impact on this type of learning. Informal learning acts as a link between research, academics, and community, "Through informal, unstructured activities students set priorities and goals, learn the value of intellectual flexibility, make choices about career paths and future learning, and decide what to do with the rest of their lives."

The Task Force (MIT 1998, Sept.) suggests that in order to develop the elements of reason, knowledge, and wisdom that characterize the educated individual, MIT cannot rely on structured learning alone. In the past, MIT used the research university model of Von Humboldt, who proposed educating students by exploiting the informal interaction between research and academic study. In the future, however, the Institute plans to have community activities play a larger educational role. Two forces are cited for this change:

> First, informal learning-by-doing through peer interaction at the community level can properly develop in students many qualities of the educated individual. Community interaction is an excellent preparation for life: paired with MIT's formal curriculum, it is a means to develop communication skills and the ability to think critically about societal issues, and it provides experience with cultural and intellectual diversity. Second, the accelerating changes of the information revolution are eroding the boundaries of place and organization. To add value to a technical education available elsewhere, MIT will increasingly have to rely on the value it can deliver by combining informal, community-based learning with structured, curriculum-based learning.

While the Institute may have some deficiencies in the area of student life, the Task Force (MIT 1998, Sept.) contends that the MIT community resembles society at large in many respects. A strength of MIT's community is the large number of student activities and groups. The dedication and commitment of students and faculty who participate in MIT community activities is impressive given the demands of research and academics. The fact that such a system has evolved at MIT is a testament to the drive and diversity of interest found at the Institute, especially considering that all activities at the Institute, including undergraduate education, revolve around the simple fact that MIT is a preeminent research university and a national and international resource. The Task Force, however, realizes that students and faculty often have little positive incentive to go beyond the Institute's academic requirements. As a result, community activities may be viewed less important. Therefore, the Task Force recommends that the Institute explore ways to give formal recognition for participation in such activities.

This summary of research from printed works and university web sites provides additional support for the hypothesis that the University of the Americas could add value and gain a competitive advantage at a national and international level through voluntary student clubs that possess official status in the University. Nevertheless, we will continue to investigate this subject and attempt to obtain empirical evidence that will either further substantiate the hypothesis or refute it.

Chapter 3

Methodology

In this chapter, the methodology utilized to obtain the empirical evidence is explained. The chapter includes information regarding the hypothesis, the constructs, the measuring instrument, the sample, the pilot test, the evaluation of the questionnaire, and the official test.

3.1 Hypothesis

In his book <u>Business Research Methods</u>, C. William Emory (1985) states that many different definitions have been given for the meaning of this term hypothesis and various types of hypotheses exist. In this thesis, the hypothesis is a statement in which variables have been assigned to a case. Emory defines a case as "the entity or thing the hypothesis talks about. The variable is the characteristic, trait or attribute which, in the hypothesis, is imputed to the case."

The hypothesis of this thesis is a "relational hypothesis" which "describes a relationship between two variables with respect to some case." More specifically, the hypothesis is an "explanatory" or "causal" type of relational hypothesis. Emory (1985) states:

> With explanatory or causal hypotheses, there is an implication that the existence of, or a change in one variable, causes or leads to an effect on the other variable. The causal variable is typically called the independent variable (IV) and the other the dependent variable (DV). "Cause" means roughly to "help make happen." That is the IV need not be the sole reason for the existence of, or change in, the DV.

The hypothesis of this thesis states, "the University of the Americas could add value and gain a competitive advantage at a national and international level through voluntary student clubs that possess official status in the University." Based on Emory's definitions, the case is the University of the Americas, the independent variable is voluntary student clubs and the dependent variables are adding value and gaining competitive advantage. According to the hypothesis, the independent variable "voluntary student clubs" will cause or lead to an effect on the dependent variables "adding value" and "gaining competitive advantage." Although the case is the University of the Americas, the effect of these voluntary student clubs will be tested at top American universities, since the University of the Americas does not allow voluntary student clubs. The results of the test will be used to offer empirical evidence to substantiate or refute the hypothesis. While the results may provide strong evidence for or against the hypothesis, the hypothesis could only be tested and proven through a real life study probably over a number of years in which voluntary study clubs actually existed on the campus of the University of the Americas.

3.2 Constructs

As defined in section 2.1 "Concepts and Terminology", adding value and gaining competitive advantage involve giving worth or increasing the worth of a product or service and gaining some type of a benefit over rival companies. In order to determine if voluntary student clubs could add value and competitive advantage, two constructs were examined. The constructs were composed of items, most of which were derived from ideas presented in section 2.5 "Literary Review". Although each item within a construct has a specific focus, all of the items are related to the phenomenon represented by the construct. While the constructs deal with two different areas, both specifically relate to the effect of voluntary student clubs.

DeVellis (1991) states:

> researchers are interested in constructs rather than items or scales per se....The underlying phenomenon or construct that a scale is intended to reflect is called the latent variable....Although we cannot observe or quantify it directly, the latent variable presumably takes on a specific value under some specified set of conditions.

In order to obtain empirical evidence for the hypothesis, the author designed an instrument to measure the positive, negative or nil effect of voluntary student clubs on a university through the two constructs. These constructs represent two areas that are critical to universities for adding value and gaining competitive advantage.

The first construct, **Student Growth**, includes ten items associated with areas specifically related to the effect of voluntary student clubs on the students.

a. Social development of students – This item deals with the process by which an individual learns the patterns of his or her culture through interaction with other individuals. This process contributes to the shaping of human behavior and permits individuals to interact positively with others and reach their human potential (Macionis 1991).

b. Developing leadership ability – This item involves the skills to direct and organize people to achieve a common objective. Leadership includes establishing a vision, motivating, encouraging, coaching, empowering, mentoring and serving (Carnegie 1993; Rosen 1996).

c. Building self-esteem – This item addresses the view that an individual has of himself or herself. It includes such things as confidence, acceptance and satisfaction with oneself. Self-esteem is essential for proper personal growth.

d. Instilling an entrepreneur spirit – This item refers to the desire to organize, manage, and assume the risks of a business or enterprise (Entrepreneur 2000). In addition, this item refers to the ability to be a visionary, a person who is able to dream, but more importantly carry out their dreams (Shefshy 1994). Colleges must attempt to do more than just prepare students to work for a company. They must also attempt to instill an entrepreneur spirit so that students will dream, be visionaries and start new businesses.

e. Assuming responsibility – This item deals with the area of dependability, reliability and specifically with accepting duties and fulfilling them. An important part of personal growth involves assuming responsibility.

f. Encouraging teamwork – This item involves collaborating with others in an effort to achieve a common goal. Effective teamwork will allow a group of individuals to accomplish more than another group of individuals working independently. Through effective teamwork, the overall performance of the group of individuals will be greater than the sum of the performances of all the individual participants (Chesla 2000).

g. Academic performance – This item deals with formal educational elements. It pertains to courses of study and grades. Most, if not all universities would consider this as one of their highest priorities and fundamental purposes for existence.

h. Promoting ethical values – This item deals with morals, standards, ideals and principles. Students must gain knowledge, but knowledge alone without ethical values can be dangerous. Universities must be concerned with not only imparting knowledge to students, but ethical values to use this knowledge properly.

i. Alumni giving – This item refers to the percentage of alumni that make financial donations to their university. The alumni giving rate is usually regarded as an indirect measure of alumni satisfaction and often used as an indicator for ranking universities.

j. Hiring decisions of companies – This item refers to the choice that businesses make whether to employ an applicant. These choices usually involve reviewing and evaluating the qualifications of the candidates, including their educational accomplishments and experiences.

The second construct, *University Growth*, includes four items associated with areas specifically related to the effect of voluntary student clubs on the university.

a. Adding value to the university – As the phrase implies, this item involves giving worth to or increasing the worth of the college. In business administration theory, adding value to the product or service is one of the most important goals for a company. This item is of particular importance since the hypothesis of this thesis is based on this concept.

b. Attracting students to the university – This item refers to the ability to draw students to the college. An indicator often utilized in ranking universities involves the university's enrollment of top high school students. Universities want to draw students, especially the best ones.

c. Retention rate of students – This item refers to the number of students at a university that graduate compared with those that drop out or transfer to another university. The ability of a university to retain students is an indicator often used in ranking universities. According the *US News* college rankings, "The higher the proportion of freshmen who return to campus the following year and eventually graduate, the better a school may be at offering the classes and services students need to succeed" (US News Online 2000).

d. Overall college experience – As the phase implies, this item means the total impression based on everything the university offers. This item closely corresponds to the idea of adding value and will be of particular importance in validating the hypothesis of this thesis.

3.3 Measuring Instrument

The measuring instrument for the survey was a questionnaire (See Appendix A). The questionnaire utilized Osgood's Semantic Differential scale. According to Emory (1985), "It is based on the proposition that an object can have several dimensions of cognitive meaning which can be located in multidimensional property space, in this case, called semantic space." This type of scale attempts to measure the psychological meanings of an object to an individual. The scale utilizes words that refer to opposite extremes of the spectrum and provides spaces along the continuum to choose a response. The scale in the questionnaire provided seven spaces that allowed the respondent to select either a negative, positive, or neutral response for each item. If the individual felt that he or she could not furnish an answer, a space was provided with the letters NR that referred to No Response.

While many different scales exist, Osgood's Semantic Differential (SD) scale appeared to be the most appropriate for the type of research conducted in this investigation. Emory (1985) states:

> In summary, the SD has a number of specific advantages. It is an effective and easy way to secure attitudes from a large sample. These attitudes may be measured in both direction and intensity. The total set of responses provides a comprehensive picture of the meaning of an object, as well as a measure of the subject doing the rating. It is a standardized technique that is easily repeated but escapes many of the problems of response distortion found with more direct methods.

In addition to the semantic scale, the questionnaire asked the respondent for some general information and included a section for comments. The comment section provided respondents with the opportunity to add any information that they felt was pertinent. Balian (1988) explains:

> in a survey questionnaire a number of qualitative open-ended, "write-in" comments may be solicited from respondents combined with questions requiring strictly numeric responses….The most powerful research projects utilize the synergy of qualitative and qualitative designs used in conjunction with each other.

3.4 The Sample

The type of sample that corresponds to this kind of research is called a judgment sample. According to Emory (1985), a judgment sample is not based on probability; instead the members are chosen because they conform to "certain criteria."

Two samples were necessary, one for the pilot test, and one for the official test. The pilot test sample consisted of six major U.S. universities that had a ranking lower than 20. The official test sample consisted of the top seven U.S. universities as listed in Table 2.0 in section 2.4. The criteria for choosing the members of both judgment samples was based on the following conditions:

1. They are faculty, staff or administrators.
2. They work in a department dealing with academic affairs, admissions, alumni affairs, career services or student affairs.

The members of the judgment samples included deans, professors, and individuals that would be regarded as experts in their field, with first-hand knowledge of voluntary student clubs. The five departments encompass a broad scope that reflects the effects of voluntary student clubs before, during, and after the students are at the university. These departments should be able to provide qualified opinions especially in several key areas:

<u>Academic Affairs</u> – the effects of participation in voluntary student clubs on academic performance.

<u>Admissions</u> – the effects of voluntary student clubs on attracting students to the university and the effect of participation in voluntary student clubs on retention rates.

<u>Alumni Affairs</u> – the effects of voluntary student clubs from the perspective of alumni and specifically in regard to alumni giving.

<u>Career Services</u> – the effects of participation in voluntary student clubs on the hiring decisions of companies.

<u>Student Affairs</u> – the effects of voluntary student clubs from the perspective of professionals whose primary function involves issues related to students.

3.5 Pilot Test

A pilot test was performed primarily to evaluate the questionnaire and explore the feasibility of using e-mail. The pilot test was e-mailed to personnel in the five previously mentioned departments at Auburn University, the University of Miami (Florida), Tulane University, Florida State University, Carnegie Mellon University, and the College of William and Mary. A total of 107 questionnaires were e-mailed and 30 questionnaires were returned, for a response rate of approximately 28 percent. This response rate was satisfactory; therefore e-mail was utilized for sending the questionnaires of the official test.

During the pilot sampling, slight changes were made to the questionnaire that seemed to improve the response rate. These changes involved reformatting the message in order to be more compatible with different types of e-mail software and clarifying to whom the questionnaire was directed. No changes were made that affected any of the items of the questions.

3.6 Internal Consistency Reliability

The responses of the pilot test were compiled and checked for internal consistency reliability. According to DeVellis (1991):

> Internal consistency reliability, as the name implies, is concerned with the homogeneity of the items comprising a scale…measurement theory suggests that the relationship among items are logically connected to the relationships of the items to the latent variable. If the items of a scale have a strong relationship to the latent variable, they will have a strong relationship to each other. Although we cannot directly observe the linkage between items and the latent variable, we can certainly determine whether the items are correlated to one another. A scale is internally consistent to the extent that its items are highly intercorrelated. High inter-item correlations suggest that the items are all measuring the same thing.

The internal consistency reliability test was performed using the computer program SPSS to determine the coefficient alpha often referred to as Cronbach's alpha. To perform this test, the semantic scale spaces were assigned the following values:

(Negative)   (Positive)
                                         NR
(1) (2) (3) (4) (5) (6) (7)   (9)

All of the questionnaire responses were converted to these numerical values (See Appendix B). The letters NR (No Response) were assigned the number 9, but excluded in the calculations. The SPSS test results (See Appendix C) indicated the following:

- For the first construct, Student Growth, the standardized item alpha was .9127, which is considered high and indicates a good level of reliability.
- For the second construct, University Growth, the standardized item alpha was .6093, which is considered somewhat low and indicates the level of reliability is minimally acceptable.
- For the combination of the two constructs the standardized item alpha was .9335, which is considered high and indicates a good level of reliability.

The alpha for the first construct and the combined constructs were slightly higher than normally expected, which probably is due to the large number of items being examined. However, these alphas are adequate and indicate that the internal consistency reliability is acceptable.

The alpha of second construct was slightly lower than normally expected, which is probably due to the several factors. First, the construct has only four items, and with fewer items there can be greater variation of the alpha. Second, the response scores were fairly high and reasonably consistent, which causes a relatively high mean and low variance resulting in a lower alpha. According to DeVellis (1991):

> Generally, items with means too near to an extreme of the response range will have low variances, and those that vary over a narrow range will correlate poorly with other items. As stated previously, an item that does not vary cannot covary. Thus either a lopsided mean or a low variance for any reason will tend to reduce an item's correlation with other items.

In regard to items with a high mean and consistent responses, DeVellis explains that on a scale from 1 to 7, "A piling up of 7, for example, would suggest that the item was not worded strongly enough (i.e., that it was rare to find anyone who would disagree with it)." However, for the purposes of this investigation, the high mean and consistent responses may not necessarily be unfavorable. The high, consistent scores may reflect a consensus of opinion and not a problem with the questions.

The SPSS program provides calculations to show if higher alphas could be obtained by deleting certain questions. According to the program, eliminating the final question would increase the alpha to .6885. This increase, however, is not substantial and a review of the question shows that eliminating it would not be advisable. The question states: "What effect do voluntary student clubs have on: The overall college experience?"

Clearly, this is a valuable question and will be of particular importance in validating the hypothesis of this thesis. Furthermore, the item is worded strongly and the scale gives respondents the opportunity to choose a range of answers. Therefore, the fact that most respondents gave a high score appears to be a sign of agreement and not the result of a bad question.

Based on these observations, the internal consistency reliability test appears satisfactory. None of the items on the questionnaire were modified for the official test. The only changes were those previously discussed.

3.7 Official Test

The official test followed the same methodology as described for the pilot test. The questionnaires were sent by e-mail to the seven benchmark universities. Since the questionnaire had no modifications to the items, a second internal consistency reliability test was not performed on the results.

Chapter 4

Analysis

In this chapter, the results of the pilot test and official test will be analyzed. First, the pilot test results will briefly be examined, then an in-depth analysis will be performed on the results of the official test of the benchmark universities.

4.1 Scale Weighted Values

In order to tabulate and analyze the responses, the semantic scale spaces were assigned the following weighted values:

(Negative)   (Positive)
                              NR
$\overline{(-3)}$ $\overline{(-2)}$ $\overline{(-1)}$ $\overline{(0)}$ $\overline{(+1)}$ $\overline{(+2)}$ $\overline{(+3)}$ $\overline{(x)}$

The lowest response score for an individual item was –3 and the highest response score for an individual item was +3. The letters NR (No Response) were not assigned a value. The average item score was calculated based on all of the responses for that item, excluding the NR responses. The average construct score was calculated based on all of the average items scores for the items in that construct. The numerical values did not appear on the questionnaire.

4.2 Pilot Test

The participant responses were converted to the weighted values (See Appendix D). The total responses, total weighted values, and average scores are shown in Table 4.1.

TABLE 4.1 PILOT TEST RESULTS										
	-3	-2	-1	0	1	2	3	NR	Total Value	Average Score
Social Development				1	1	15	13		30	
Weighted Values	0	0	0	0	1	30	39		70	2.33
Leadership				2	7	8	13		30	
Weighted Values	0	0	0	0	7	16	39		62	2.07
Self-esteem				1	11	8	10		30	
Weighted Values	0	0	0	0	11	16	30		57	1.90
Entrepeneur Spirit			1	10	6	5	5	3	27	
Weighted Values	0	0	-1	0	6	10	15		30	1.11
Responsibility				4	7	12	7		30	
Weighted Values	0	0	0	0	7	24	21		52	1.73
Teamwork					9	9	12		30	
Weighted Values	0	0	0	0	9	18	36		63	2.10
Academics			1	13	9	2	3	2	28	
Weighted Values	0	0	-1	0	9	4	9		21	0.75
Ethical Values			2	7	5	6	5	5	25	
Weighted Values	0	0	-2	0	5	12	15		30	1.20
Alumni giving		1		8	1	2	7	11	19	
Weighted Values	0	-2	0	0	1	4	21		24	1.26
Hiring decisions				2	8	7	8	5	25	
Weighted Values	0	0	0	0	8	14	24		46	1.84
Attracting Students				2	9	7	8	4	26	
Weighted Values	0	0	0	0	9	14	24		47	1.81
Retention rate				5	9	5	8	3	27	
Weighted Values	0	0	0	0	9	10	24		43	1.59
Adding Value					5	14	10	1	29	
Weighted Values	0	0	0	0	5	28	30		63	2.17
Overall Experience					1	14	15		30	
Weighted Values	0	0	0	0	1	28	45		74	2.47

Prepared by author using data from Appendix D.

The items in Table 4.1 are listed as they appeared on the questionnaire. The rows with the item name show the total number of responses for each space on the scale for that item. The rows below each item labeled "Weighted Values" show the total weighted value for each space on the scale for that item. The assigned weights are listed at the top of the columns. The column "Total Value" provides the total number of responses and the total weighted score for each item. The column "Average Score" shows the average weighted response for each item. The calculations did not include the NR column.

The average item scores are listed in ascending order in Table 4.2. All of the scores were in the positive range, indicating that the respondents in general considered voluntary student clubs as having a positive effect on each item in the survey.

TABLE 4.2 PILOT TEST ITEM SCORES	
Item	Average Score
The overall college experience	2.47
Social development of the students	2.33
Adding value to the university	2.17
Encouraging teamwork	2.10
Developing leadership ability	2.07
Building of self-esteem	1.90
The hiring decisions of companies	1.84
Attracting students to the university	1.81
Assuming responsibility	1.73
The retention rate of students	1.59
Alumni giving	1.26
Promoting ethical values	1.20
Instilling an entrepreneur spirit	1.07
Academic performance	0.75

Prepared by author using data from Table 4.1.

The construct scores are shown in Table 4.3. Each construct had a high score in the positive range indicating that the respondents in general considered voluntary student clubs as having a positive effect on both student growth and university growth.

The pilot test was performed primarily to check the reliability of the questionnaire and explore the feasibility of using e-mail to conduct the survey. Sections 3.5 "Pilot Test" and 3.6 "Internal Consistency Reliability" provide additional information about the pilot test including the universities in the sample and the results of the internal consistency reliability test. Since the universities in the pilot test are not considered benchmark universities, the results are not mentioned in the conclusions of the thesis.

TABLE 4.3 PILOT TEST CONSTRUCT SCORES		
Item	Average Score	Average Construct Score
Social development of the students	2.33	Student Growth 1.63
Encouraging teamwork	2.10	
Developing leadership ability	2.07	
Building of self-esteem	1.90	
The hiring decisions of companies	1.84	
Assuming responsibility	1.73	
Alumni giving	1.26	
Promoting ethical values	1.20	
Instilling an entrepreneur spirit	1.07	
Academic performance	0.75	
The overall college experience	2.47	Universty Growth 2.01
Adding value to the university	2.17	
Attracting students to the university	1.81	
The retention rate of students	1.59	

Prepared by author using information from section 3.2 and data from Table 4.2.

4.3 Official Test

The official test was sent by e-mail to a judgment sample of the benchmark universities. A total of 444 questionnaires were sent and 96 questionnaires were returned. Of the 96 questionnaires returned, 91 were usable and five were unusable. The percentage rate of usable questionnaires returned was 20.5%. The individual statistics for each participant that responded with a usable questionnaire are shown in Appendix E.

A summary of the participants by gender and age group is shown in Table 4.4. A total of 58 (63.7%) women and 33 (36.3%) men returned usable questionnaires. The most responses of any group came from women age 40-49, returning a total of 17 questionnaires. The most responses by men came from the 50+ age group, returning a total of 14 questionnaires. The most combined responses of both men and women came from the 50+ age group, returning a total of 30 questionnaires. The fewest responses for both men and women came from the 20-29 age group, returning a total of 13 questionnaires. The majority of the responses came from men and women in the 40-49 and 50+ age groups. These groups returned a combined total of 56 questionnaires or about 62 % of the total responses.

TABLE 4.4 OFFICIAL TEST PARTICIPANT DATA SUMMARY			
Category	Men	Women	Total
Age 20-29	3	10	13
Age 30-39	7	15	22
Age 40-49	9	17	26
Age 50+	14	16	30
Totals	33	58	91

Prepared by the author using data from Appendix E.

Figure 4.1 provides a graphic of the number of men and women participants by age groups.

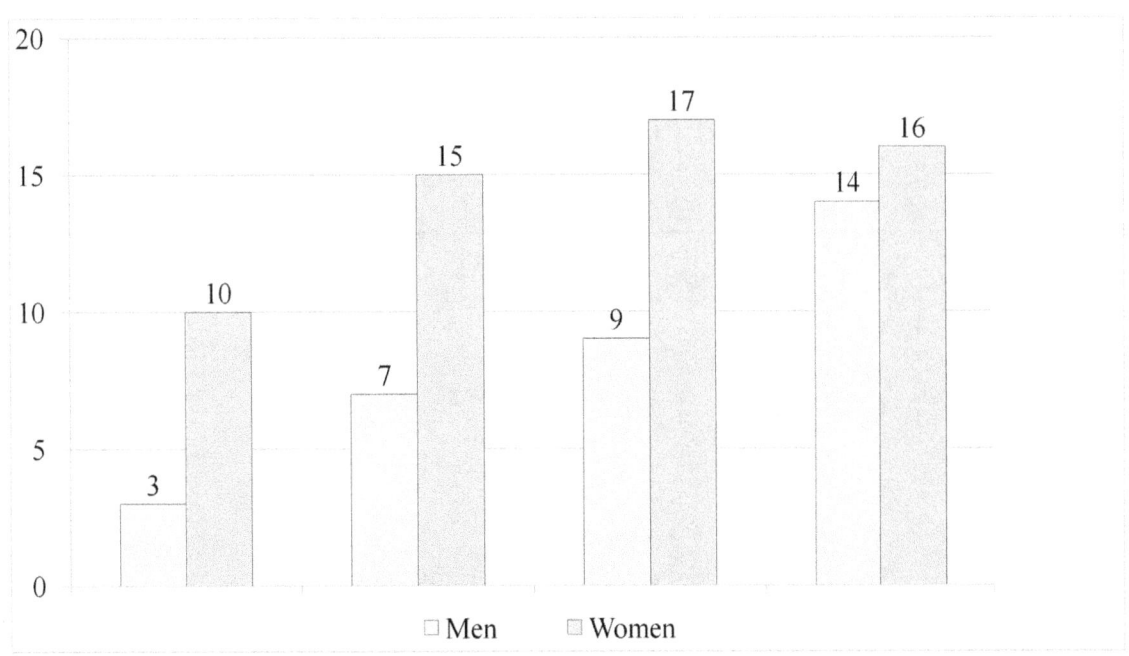

Figure 4.1
Official Test Participant Categories
Prepared by the author using data from Table 4.4

Figure 4.2 and 4.3 provide a graphic of the number of years that participants have worked at the university and in the field of education. The dots indicate the total years of experience of each participant and the line indicates the average number of years for all participants. The average number of years that the participants worked at their university was 10.69. The average number of years that the participants worked in the field of education was 15.61. This information indicates that the participants of the sample have ample experience working at their university as well as in the field of education.

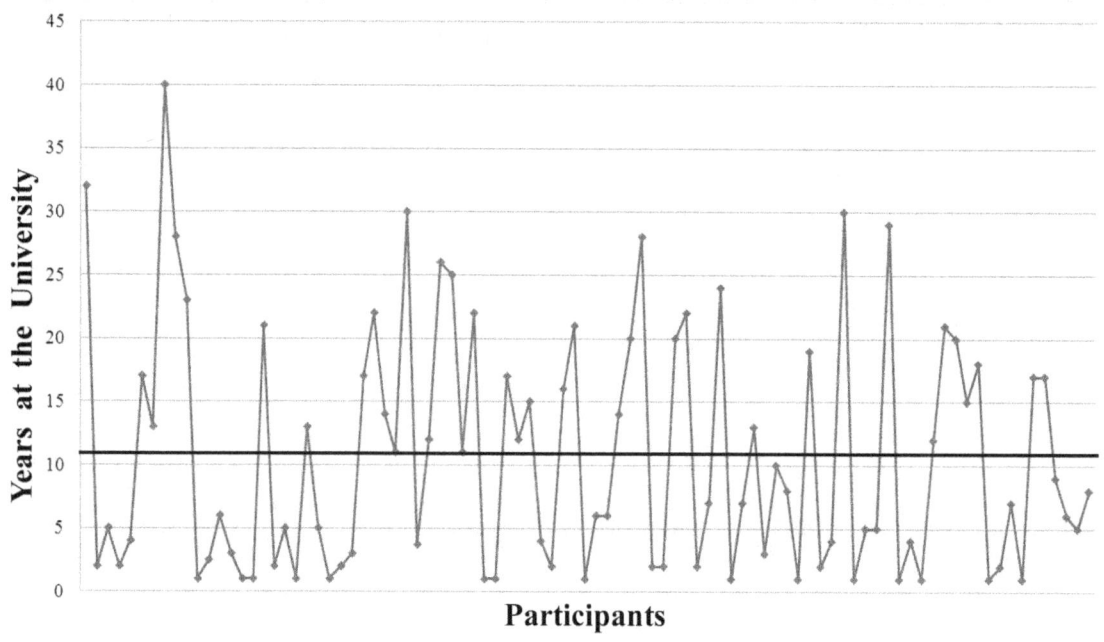

Figure 4.2
Official Test University Experience
Prepared by the author using data from Appendix E.

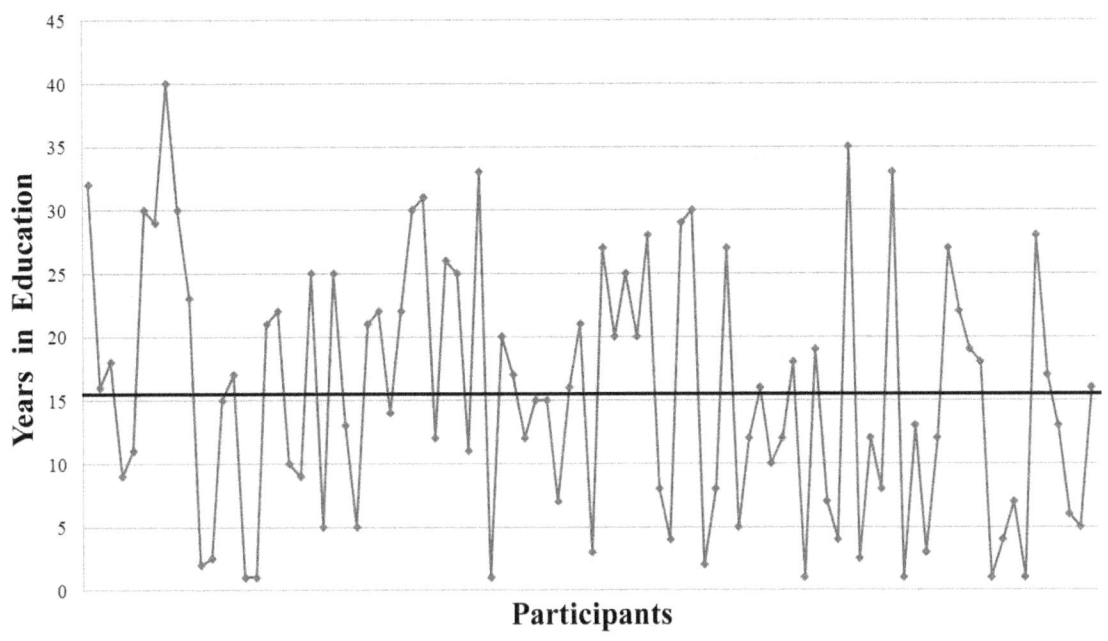

Figure 4.3
Official Test Education Experience
Prepared by the author using data from Appendix E.

The total number of usable responses by university and department are shown in Table 4.5.

TABLE 4.5 OFFICIAL TEST TOTAL RESPONSES						
University Name	Academic Affairs	Admissions	Alumni Affairs	Career Services	Student Affairs	Totals
Princeton	2	0	2	0	2	6
Harvard	2	2	3	1	5	13
Yale	4	3	1	0	2	10
CalTech	1	1	3	3	3	11
MIT	4	1	2	6	3	16
Stanford	6	0	4	3	4	17
Penn	5	2	3	4	4	18
Totals	24	9	18	17	23	91

Prepared by author using information provided by official test respondents.

The University of Pennsylvania had the highest number of responses with 18, while Princeton University had the lowest with six. The area of academic affairs had the highest number of total responses with 24. This high number was partly due to the large number of people in this area and their contact information being readily available. The lowest response was from admissions, with a total of nine. Several people in admissions replied that they could not answer the survey since they had limited involvement with students. These replies may help to explain the reason for the overall low response from admissions. The area most willing to respond was student affairs. Although many of these departments had a small staff, a high percent of them responded. A total of 23 responses were received from student affairs, while the fewest number of surveys were sent to this area. The wide variety of responses from different areas and universities assures a well-rounded sample, which helps to eliminate bias.

Figure 4.4 provides a graphic of the total number of responses by area with the corresponding percentages.

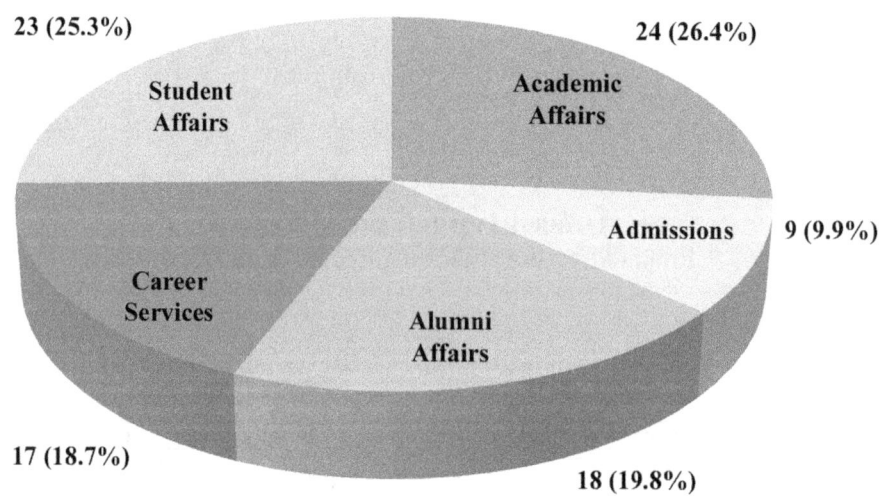

Figure 4.4
Official Test Total Responses
Prepared by the author using data from Table 4.5

4.4 Interpretation

This section examines the results of the official test and reviews comments that were provided by the participants. Selected comments from the survey participants have been included where they seemed most appropriate. While the names of the participants providing comments have been kept anonymous, the university where they are employed has been given. All of these participants met the criteria of the judgment sample described in Section 3.4 "The Sample."

Since the questionnaire was fairly general, some of the participants commented that it was difficult to answer the questions. One participant from Princeton stated:

> I realize that your survey is designed to make responding easy, but almost all of your categories could elicit a different response depending on just what the student/volunteer group is. Ideally, a good student/volunteer group would create a positive experience for both the institution and the students, but there are certainly examples of volunteer groups, even those created with the best of intentions, that can have quite the opposite effect.

This comment is certainly valid. The questionnaire designed was to be user-friendly and intended to be quick and easy to answer in order to help achieve a high response rate. The purpose of the questionnaire was to obtain empirical evidence on the overall effect of voluntary student clubs that would substantiate or refute the hypothesis. It was not designed to collect detailed information on individual clubs. Since the participant completed and returned the questionnaire, she apparently understood the general nature of the survey.

As explained in section 4.1, the participant responses were converted to the weighted values (See Appendix F). The total responses, total weighted values, and average scores are shown in Table 4.6. The items are listed in the order that they appeared in the questionnaire. Table 4.6 follows the same format that was explained in section 4.2 for Table 4.1. A brief examination of Table 4.6 reveals that the vast majority of the responses for each item were positive with only a small minority of the responses being negative.

TABLE 4.6 OFFICIAL TEST RESULTS

	-3	-2	-1	0	1	2	3	NR	Total Value	Average Score
Social Development	0	0	1	2	10	35	42	1	90	
Weighted Values	0	0	-1	0	10	70	126		205	2.28
Leadership	0	0	0	3	17	29	41	1	90	
Weighted Values	0	0	0	0	17	58	123		198	2.20
Self-esteem	0	0	1	5	23	26	35	1	90	
Weighted Values	0	0	-1	0	23	52	105		179	1.99
Entrepeneur Spirit	0	0	6	19	24	18	14	10	81	
Weighted Values	0	0	-6	0	24	36	42		96	1.19
Responsibility	0	0	2	5	21	32	28	3	88	
Weighted Values	0	0	-2	0	21	64	84		167	1.90
Teamwork	0	0	1	6	17	30	37	0	91	
Weighted Values	0	0	-1	0	17	60	111		187	2.05
Academics	0	4	11	31	22	10	4	9	82	
Weighted Values	0	-8	-11	0	22	20	12		35	0.43
Ethical Values	0	0	6	28	18	20	8	11	80	
Weighted Values	0	0	-6	0	18	40	24		76	0.95
Alumni giving	0	0	0	14	24	23	6	24	67	
Weighted Values	0	0	0	0	24	46	18		88	1.31
Hiring decisions	0	0	2	11	21	26	12	19	72	
Weighted Values	0	0	-2	0	21	52	36		107	1.49
Attracting Students	0	0	4	14	17	24	17	15	76	
Weighted Values	0	0	-4	0	17	48	51		112	1.47
Retention rate	0	2	6	11	20	22	14	16	75	
Weighted Values	0	-4	-6	0	20	44	42		96	1.28
Adding Value	0	0	3	2	15	30	40	1	90	
Weighted Values	0	0	-3	0	15	60	120		192	2.13
Overall Experience	0	0	1	1	13	33	43	0	91	
Weighted Values	0	0	-1	0	13	66	129		207	2.27

Prepared by author using data from Appendix F.

The average item scores listed in ascending order are shown in Table 4.7 and the construct scores are shown in Table 4.8.

TABLE 4.7 OFFICIAL TEST ITEM SCORES

Item	Average Score
Social development of the students	2.28
The overall college experience	2.27
Developing leadership ability	2.20
Adding value to the university	2.13
Encouraging teamwork	2.05
Building of self-esteem	1.99
Assuming responsibility	1.90
The hiring decisions of companies	1.49
Attracting students to the university	1.47
Alumni giving	1.31
The retention rate of students	1.28
Instilling an entrepreneur spirit	1.19
Promoting ethical values	0.95
Academic performance	0.43

Prepared by author using data from Table 4.6.

TABLE 4.8 OFFICIAL TEST CONSTRUCT SCORES

Item	Average Score	Average Construct Score
Social development of the students	2.28	
Developing leadership ability	2.20	
Encouraging teamwork	2.05	
Building of self-esteem	1.99	
Assuming responsibility	1.90	Student Growth 1.58
The hiring decisions of companies	1.49	
Alumni giving	1.31	
Instilling an entrepreneur spirit	1.19	
Promoting ethical values	0.95	
Academic performance	0.43	
The overall college experience	2.27	
Adding value to the university	2.13	University Growth 1.79
Attracting students to the university	1.47	
The retention rate of students	1.28	

Prepared by the author using information from section 3.2 and data from Table 4.7.

All of the total item scores in the both constructs were in the positive range, indicating that the respondents in general considered voluntary student clubs as having a positive effect on each of the items. Both construct scores were in the positive range and relatively high, indicating that the respondents in general considered voluntary student clubs as having a strong positive effect on both student growth and university growth. The following analysis examines each item using the data in Tables 4.6, 4.7 and 4.8:

Student Growth Construct

a. Social development of students – This item received the highest score in the construct with +2.28. It had the highest overall score of items in both constructs. This item also had the most +3 responses in the construct, with a total of 42. A total of 87 participants responded positively, one participant responded negatively, two claimed no effect, and one chose no response. A participant from University of Pennsylvania comments, "these extra activities give a person the chance to expand their lives, their friends, their responsibilities, try different experiences, see if they like leading a group, working with a group, helping others, etc. So for the most part I believe they are positive."

b. Developing leadership ability – This item received a score of +2.20. It was one of only two items that received no negative response. A total of 87 participants responded positively, three participants claimed no effect, and one chose no response. This item also received a number of positive comments. For example, a participant from MIT states that involvement in voluntary student clubs, "helps students develop leadership skills and life skills they will need after leaving college."

c. Encouraging teamwork – This item received a score of +2.05. It is the only item in the construct where all of the participants responded. A total of 84 participants responded positively, one responded negatively, and six claimed no effect. In regard to this item and clubs in general, a participant from Harvard explains:

> Involvement in clubs and activities is an important way for students to connect to other students in the University or College and to get involved in issues or areas that interest them. The connections they make through these clubs can lead to job interest, contacts and relationships with other classmates. In my opinion, it is far better to be a well rounded person th[a]n to get straight A's. The ability to network and get involved can have an important impact on the how the student takes these skills into the world after graduation.

d. Building self-esteem – This item received a score of +1.99. A total of 84 participants responded positively, one responded negatively, five claimed no effect, and one chose no response. A participant from California Institute of Technology comments:

> I think, in the long [run], joining a club ultimately allows a student to apply academic knowledge and skills to everyday life experiences. Active involvement helps students widen their circle of friends and allows them to create a sense of purpose on a campus. The only drawback I see is that students can use over involvement as a means to procrastinate.

e. Assuming responsibility – This item received a score of +1.90. A total of 81 participants responded positively, two responded negatively, five claimed no effect, and three chose no response. With regard to this item and clubs in general, a participant from MIT states:

> The answers depend on several variables including level of responsibility and engagement in any given student club. The potential [exists] for character development, etc., through membership, and especially leadership, in/of this kind of opportunity. But one could also join, and participate minimally, and/or have a bad, or non-experience. So, great enhancement is possible but not a sure thing.

f. Hiring decisions of companies – This item received a score of +1.49. A total of 59 participants responded positively, two responded negatively, 11 claimed no effect, and 19 chose no response. From the high number of no responses, many of the participants obviously did not feel qualified to provide a definite answer. However, several participants made strong positive comments regarding this item. A participant from Stanford University states:

> Student clubs and activities are becoming increasingly important to employers. Student's academic achievements are becoming equal as more and more students receive high marks. Employers are now turning to extra curricular activities to set students apart from each other.

Another participant from MIT explains:

EQ, Emotional Intelligence has recently become a hot topic in today's business environment. The development of emotional/behavioral competence is a necessary compliment to IQ in most leadership and managerial positions. My expressed belief is that some of the social interaction that takes place in club activities can begin to build some of the emotional competence needed to be successful in today's workplace. In fact, recent studies show that EQ is attributed to 80% of real world success in the workplace. The other 20% is attributed to IQ.

g. Alumni giving – This item received a score of +1.31. It was one of only two items that received no negative response. A total of 53 participants responded positively, 11 claimed no effect, and 24 chose no response. The number of no responses was the highest for any item in either construct. Therefore, many of the participants did not feel qualified to provide a definite answer. Several participants, however, made strong positive comments regarding this item. A participant from Yale states:

> As alumni, students are more likely to give to the College and are more likely to maintain strong affective ties to the College if his/her experience in extracurricular activities was positive. These (outside of classroom experiences) are the ones that stay in student's minds long after they've graduated.

Another participant from MIT comments, "We have seen in talking to alumni that they feel more connected to their alma mater through their co-curricular activities. We see a lot of donations directed to student groups due to the positive experience involved students had while in college."

h. Instilling an entrepreneur spirit – This item received a score of +1.19. A total of 52 participants responded positively, six participants responded negatively, 19 claimed no effect, and 10 chose no response. In regard to this item, several participants commented that the type of club was a factor. A participant from Harvard stated, "I think this depends on the nature of the club. Clubs that are organized around a political, social activism, or business purpose develop this characteristic far more strongly than social or athletic clubs."

i. Promoting ethical values – This item received a score of +0.95. A total of 46 participants responded positively, six responded negatively, 28 claimed no effect, and 11 chose no response. A participant from Yale comments:

> The out-of-classroom experience--insofar as a student's involvement in being part of or leading a student organization--is equally as important and compliments well a student's academic pursuits. A student's involvement in such organizations teaches them to think independently, to forge his/her own identity, values, and ethics at the same time it teaches him/her to work as part of a larger collective...The friendships made in one's participation in student activities and the life's experiences learned therein is what shapes the individual and what allows him/her to make the necessary connections between what one is learning

in class with what one learns about him/herself through his/her relationships with others.

j. Academic performance – This item received the lowest score of any item in either constructs with +0.43. A total of 36 participants responded positively, 15 responded negatively, 31 claimed no effect, and nine chose no response. The 31 participants claiming no effect were the most for any item in either construct. The 15 participants responding negatively were the most for any item in either construct. Nevertheless, this item received a positive total score. A participant from MIT that felt strongly about the positive effect states:

> For most students voluntary membership in co-curricular activities promotes better time management skills which help academic performance. In rare instances if a student over commits themselves their involvement m[a]y hurt their academics. At MIT our students thrive on involvement in many activities and it helps them focus on all aspects of their lives. Also many students use student group involvement to supplement classroom learning.

University Growth Construct

a. Overall college experience – This item received the highest score in the construct with +2.27. It had the second highest overall score of items in both constructs. This item also had the most +3 responses of any item in the either construct with a total of 43. It is the only item in the construct where all of the participants responded. It had the highest number of participants responding positively of any item in the either construct with 89. Of the remaining two participants, one claimed no effect and one chose no response. A participant from MIT that responded positively to the survey comments, "I am also a recent graduate of MIT and I feel I know first hand what the clubs and organizations have to contribute to the community."

b. Adding value to the university – This item received a score of +2.13. It had the fourth highest overall score of items for both constructs. This item specifically relates to the hypothesis of this thesis. A total of 85 participants responded positively, three responded negatively, two claimed no effect, and one chose no response.

c. Attracting students to the university – This item received a score of +1.47. A total of 85 participants responded positively, three responded negatively, two claimed no effect, and one chose no response. A participant from University of Pennsylvania states:

> Some of these were tough to say. I've seen clubs and activities be the focal point for students be both a positive (i.e., the thing that makes them feel connected to their

college experience) and a negative (either taking too much time from studies, or the involvement is so deep and emotional that it becomes a distraction rather than an enhancement). Overall, though, from a recruiter's standpoint, the opportunity to get involved or learn about different kinds of activities is a huge draw for most young adults, and once they are here, they provide wonderful chances for personal development.

d. Retention rate of students – This item received a score of +1.28. A total of 56 participants responded positively, eight responded negatively, 11 claimed no effect, and 16 chose no response. The retention rate often is considered an important factor in determining student satisfaction with the university.

A comment from a participant at Harvard provides an example of the tremendous effect of a voluntary student organization. He states:

> The Phillips Brooks House Association (PBHA) is a student run non-profit organization that currently operates 80 programs in the Greater Boston area. These programs range from urban summer camps to the only student-run shelter for the homeless in the country. In the last year, our 1800 undergraduate volunteers have touched (and have in turn been touched by) the lives of 10,000 children and adults. PBHA is a unique manifestation of college students' idealism, energy and initiative.
>
> Founded in 1900 as the Service Committee of the Phillips Brooks House and renamed Phillips Brooks House Association in 1904, the Association has served the community in diverse ways from its origins as a religiously oriented settlement house. The creativity of PBHA students has often provided innovative models to the human service community. In the 1950's, PBHA volunteers were pioneers in working with the mentally ill and incarcerated. In the 1960's, PBHA developed a volunteer teacher's program in Africa called the Tanganyika Project that became the model in the creation of the Peace Corps.
>
> Alumni of Phillips Brooks House have gone on to be leaders in their respective fields and include such distinguished individuals as Justice David Souter, Yo Yo Ma, Dr. Robert Coles, Franklin Delano Roosevelt and countless leaders in communities across America. PBHA has often been described as "the best course at Harvard".

In regard to the overall impact of voluntary student clubs, a comment from a participant at Yale University emphasizes the positive effect of these clubs. He states that the questions seemed "self-evident" and declares:

most administrators at good colleges in the U.S., anyway, would say that clubs have a positive effect all the way down the line. There are close to 600 clubs and organizations of various kinds at Yale College, serving its undergraduate population of 5300. The school invests a fair amount of its resources in support of all those organizations because their worth isn't something we even question.

4.5 Confidence Levels

In order to calculate the confidence level of the student growth construct, the following formula was applied:

Z = 1.65
s = 0.576
e = 0.1

N = Z^2 * s^2 / e^2
N = 1.65 * 1.65 * 0.576 * 0.576 / 0.1 * 0.1
N = 2.7225 * 0.3318 / 0.01
N = 0.9033 / 0.01
N = 90.326

Z is the confidence level accuracy rate for the standard normal distribution, s is the standard deviation of the scores in the student growth construct, e is the error rate, and N is the number of participants needed in the sample. With a 90% confidence level accuracy rate and 10% error rate Z equals 1.65 and e equals 0.1. The standard deviation of the student growth construct scores equals 0.576. Since the value of N calculates to 90.326 and the total number of participants was 91, a confidence level of 90% can be assumed for the survey responses of the student growth construct.

In order to calculate the confidence level of the university growth construct, the same formula was applied, however, the value for s the standard deviation of the university growth construct scores equals 0.4247. The value for Z the confidence level accuracy rate remained 1.65 and e the error rate remained 0.1.

The university growth construct formula:

Z = 1.65
s = 0.4208
e = 0.1

N = Z^2 * s^2 / e^2

N = 1.65 * 1.65 * 0.4208 * 0.421 / 0.1 * 0.1
N = 2.7225 * 0.1771 / 0.01
N = 0.48208 / 0.01
N = 48.208

Since the value of *N* calculated to 48.208 and the total number of participants was 91, a confidence level of greater than 90% can be assumed for the survey responses of the university growth construct.

These formulas demonstrate that the survey had a sufficient number of participants in the sample to be valid. The confidence level for each construct was above 90%, which is considered satisfactory. The margin of error for each construct was less than 10%.

Chapter 5

Conclusions

This chapter reviews the evidence presented in this thesis and draws a final conclusion regarding the validity of the hypothesis. In addition, the chapter provides an explanation for the phenomenon of voluntary student clubs based on business administration theory, and areas for further research are suggested.

5.1 Summary of Research

The history of voluntary student clubs provides a glimpse of the impact that these clubs have had on students and universities over the centuries. From humble beginnings, voluntary student clubs have emerged to play an important part in U.S. universities. Whether through Christian religious clubs, literary clubs, academic clubs, artistic clubs, political clubs, international clubs or other areas of interest, students have organized themselves in groups that have provided companionship, nurtured ideas, and encouraged involvement. Often these groups have been a training ground outside the classroom that have complimented the formal classroom curriculum.

The benchmark universities acknowledge that voluntary student clubs are an important part of the educational process. These top universities have well-established policies to promote and foster the development of these clubs. The universities bestow the honor of official recognition to clubs, provide them with space on the university server for club web pages, and grant them privileges such as the use of university facilities for club activities. Furthermore, many of the benchmark universities have invested in state-of-the-art facilities specifically aimed at increasing and enhancing campus life and student involvement.

In the literary review, experts in the field of education emphasized the importance of student involvement in the educational process. Research indicates that extracurricular activities such as voluntary student clubs promote involvement, as well as improve campus life and increase the amount of time that students spend on campus. Many experts believe that the amount of time students spend on campus has a direct correlation to the effectiveness of the overall learning experience. In addition, studies suggest that extracurricular activities contribute to both higher retention rates and the personal development of students. Research also indicates that employers view participation in voluntary student clubs as positive.

Through the survey, empirical evidence was obtained from the benchmark universities that supported the hypothesis. Each construct had a high, positive score, indicating that the respondents in general considered voluntary student clubs as having a positive effect on both student growth and university growth. In fact, all 10 items in the student growth construct and all four items in the university construct had positive scores. The item, "adding value to the university" which specifically related to the hypothesis, received one of the highest scores. In addition, the comments provided by the survey participants were mainly positive. Many of the participants described in detail specific benefits of voluntary student clubs.

Based on historical facts, the practices of the benchmark universities, observations from experts in the field of education, and the empirical evidence of the survey, the hypothesis appears to have sufficient support to be considered valid. Therefore, the findings of this thesis conclude that the University of the Americas could add value and gain a competitive advantage at a national and international level through voluntary student clubs that possess official status in the university. This hypothesis however, could only be proven through a real life study, probably over a number of years in which voluntary study clubs actually existed on the campus of the University of the Americas.

5.2 The Phenomenon of Voluntary Student Clubs

While many different reasons may exist for the phenomenon of voluntary student clubs, this thesis offers an explanation from the field of business administration, specifically from the area of "service marketing." Universities are service providers because education is a service. Actually, universities often provide a wide array of services in addition to education. Some of these services include health service, career services, building maintenance, and campus security.

In recent years, business administration theory has started to place more emphasis on the marketing of services. Previous business administration theory focused primarily on the marketing of products and usually applied the same theories to services. However, services and products are not the same and new theories are emerging as a growing number of companies are performing services.

Unlike companies that market and sell a physical product, service companies provide something that is intangible. Services include such things as movies, where the customers are basically purchasing an experience; dry-cleaning, where customers are paying for a process; and consulting, where customers are paying for time and advice. Some companies market and sell a combination of a service and a product such as restaurants. However, true service companies provide no physical product, but only an intangible service. Therefore, the main challenge that service companies face is marketing something that is intangible.

In order to market a service effectively, the company must have a clear understanding of what their service means or its "reality" to the market. Understanding and defining the reality of a service requires utilizing "the tools and skills of psychology, sociology, and other behavioral sciences – tools that in product marketing usually come into play in determining image, rather than fundamental 'reality' "(Shostack 1984).

A company marketing a product often attempts to enhance its product by creating an abstract image. Service companies, however, are already offering something that is abstract and therefore usually attempt to enhance their service by creating a tangible reality. According to Shostack, the way a service company creates a tangible reality "appears to be shaped to a large extent by the things that the consumer can comprehend with his five senses." As a consumer attempts to judge a service, the service will be known primarily by "the tangible clues, the tangible evidence, that surround it." Therefore, service marketing relies on peripheral clues to communicate the reality while in product marketing, the product itself is the tangible evidence.

Many different types of services exist and some services have the advantage of being more tangible or real than others. Education, however, is a service that is usually regarded as highly intangible. Therefore, universities must attempt to make education more tangible (Shostack1984).

One way that a university can create a tangible reality for students is by promoting campus life. In order for a university to promote campus life, it must provide the necessary resources and supporting services. Although these resources and services are not the fundamental purpose for the existence of the university, they play an important part in helping to promote student involvement, which creates a tangible reality and adds value to the educational experience.

According to Grönroos (1990), most service companies provide a service package that consists of three groups of services:

- Core services – the reason for being on the market.
- Facilitating services – the services that facilitate or make possible the use of the core service.
- Supporting services – the services that increase the value of the service.

While the core service is the reason or purpose of the company, service companies must offer a service package that includes facilitating services and supporting services. Grönroos (1990) states:

> From a managerial point of view it is important to make a distinction between facilitating and supporting services. Facilitating services are mandatory. If they are left out, the service package collapses. . .The supporting services, however, are used as a means of competition only. If they are lacking, the core service can still be used nevertheless. However, the total service package may be less attractive and perhaps less competitive.

For a university, the core service is education, but in order for this core service to be used by the public, facilitating services are needed such as admissions, financial aid, etc. The supporting services would include departments such as student services. One of the ways that the department of student services can make the service package more competitive and attractive is through a voluntary student club system that enhances campus life.

All of the benchmark universities examined in this thesis have well-established supporting services that promote voluntary student clubs and campus life. These supporting services add value and competitive advantage to the university's core service of education. According to Collier (1994), the supporting services are often the "key" to differentiating from competitors and gaining competitive advantage. In addition, although a voluntary student club system may be considered merely a supporting service, the findings of this thesis demonstrate that clubs actually provide training outside of the classroom that complements the core service of education.

5.3 Further Research

It has been said that a good thesis will often raise more questions than it will answer. This thesis was directed at answering one question specifically whether the University of the Americas could add value and gain a competitive advantage at a national and international level through voluntary student clubs that possess official status in the university. Hopefully, the thesis has sufficiently answered this question and stimulated additional questions related to the topic of voluntary student clubs.

Since this thesis had a specific focus, it was not able to address many important issues related to voluntary student clubs. Further investigation is needed in many different areas in various fields. Some important areas for additional investigation are presented in the following paragraphs.

From a business standpoint, in order to justify starting a voluntary student club system, the costs must be analyzed and compared with the projected return on the investment. More research is needed to calculate the cost that the university will incur as well as the return on the investment to the university. While it may be virtually impossible to calculate the exact totals, some rough figure should be obtainable.

One of the concerns at the University of the Americas in regard to starting a voluntary student club system is the cost of hiring additional staff and faculty that may be required to direct the clubs (Mtro. Eduardo Lastra, Vice Rector of Student Affairs, Personal Interview, Nov. 4, 1998). Research is needed to analyze the costs of starting a voluntary student club system. In addition to administrative costs, other costs may be involved, including investment in additional facilities to accommodate clubs, additional computer server space to store club web pages, and additional monetary funds to provide clubs with financial assistance.

While the university may need to hire additional staff or faculty to supervise the clubs, the university may also be able to save money by receiving services from the students at no charge. For example, a bowling club, ski club, or chess club would most likely provide some instruction and training to new members and would therefore be providing educational services for which the university may not need to hire an instructor.

According to service marketing theory, an important part in the production and delivery of a service often involves customer participation. Service companies often utilize the customer to make their service more competitive. Kelley, Donnelly, & Skinner (1990) state, "When the service customer does provide resources to the service organization, the provision of these resources generally results in the customer receiving some benefit such as lower prices, greater convenience, or faster service."

In regard to customer participation, Sasser (1984) states:

The more the consumer does, the lower the labor requirements of the producer. Bag-'em-yourself groceries, salad bars at restaurants, self-service gas pumps, customer-filled-out insurance forms, and cook-it-yourself restaurants are all examples of increased consumer participation in the production of services.

In the case of a university, the students are the customers that can provide services, which could reduce costs and enhance the educational experience. Universities should consider the students in voluntary student clubs, or at least their leaders, as a part of the university workforce. According to Kelley, Donnelly, & Skinner (1990): "Although customers do not think of themselves as members of service organizations, for the purposes of service management, service organizations should actually view such customers as organizational members or 'partial employees.'"

Human resource management usually focuses on paid employees giving little attention to voluntary or partial employees. For companies that provide services, however, the management of these employees must be clearly understood. The methods for managing partial employees involve different factors than paid employees. For example, motivation of a paid employee may be purely monetary, whereas the motivation of a voluntary employee may be based on factors such as self-satisfaction, social concerns, etc. As a result, the business administrator faces different challenges in motivating these two types of employees. An area for further investigation is practices and strategies to effectively manage and utilize this potentially large voluntary student workforce.

Additional research is also required to calculate the financial benefits of voluntary student clubs in other areas. As this thesis has already demonstrated, voluntary student clubs, besides attracting students to the university, have a positive effect on the retention rate of students. However, further research is needed to estimate the expected increase in the retention rate of students and the expected increase in new students at the university. The estimated increase in both the retention rate of students and new students could then be translated into potential revenues.

The thesis found that participation in voluntary student clubs had a positive effect on the hiring decisions of companies. In addition, the thesis has shown that participation in voluntary student clubs has a positive effect on alumni giving. Therefore, alumni that participated in voluntary student clubs appear more likely to be successfully employed and willing to donate to the university. Furthermore, since the thesis demonstrated that voluntary student clubs have a positive effect on the overall college experience and add value to the university, even students that did not participate in voluntary student clubs may be positively affected in the area of alumni giving. More research is required to determine the amount of alumni giving that can be attributed to voluntary student clubs.

An area in which it may be impossible to calculate the financial value is student growth and development. As demonstrated in the thesis, some of the positive effects of voluntary student clubs on students include social development, leadership ability, teamwork, self-esteem, responsibility, an entrepreneur spirit, ethical values and academics. An interesting concept to consider is that alumni can essentially be viewed as the finished product of the university. Well-educated and successful alumni who excel in their professional, social, and civil life are a great source of marketing and publicity for the university. Therefore, providing a better educational experience not only benefits the students, but also the university. Additional research is needed to estimate the marketing value for the university that can be attributed to successful alumni.

The concept of networking has received considerable attention in recent years. Networking is being utilized in job searching, sales, and almost every area of business and social life. Voluntary student clubs may provide a place for students to learn and improve their networking skills. Also, voluntary student clubs may actually provide a means whereby students and alumni can effectively network. Further research is needed on the effect of voluntary student clubs in the area of networking.

From an educational standpoint, perhaps no cost is too high to increase student growth, improve the retention rate, attract students to the university, etc. However, this thesis was written from the standpoint of business administration. As a business, the University of the Americas must consider the costs of a voluntary student club system and the potential additional revenues the University would receive that would justify these costs. While a voluntary student club system may provide many benefits to the students and the University, the final decision must be made based on criteria that will ensure the profitability and financial solvency of the institution. From the information presented in this thesis, voluntary student clubs appear to provide a good return on investment. Nevertheless, further research is needed in this area.

     Finally, the findings of this thesis indicate overwhelmingly that voluntary student clubs have a strong, positive influence on students as well as the university. However, further research is required to determine if voluntary student clubs have negative effects, and if so, what type of negative effects. If negative effects exist, they would also need to be translated in terms of costs and lost revenues.

Chapter 6

Recommendations

In this chapter, recommendations are given for developing policies to begin a voluntary student club system at the University of the Americas. These recommendations are based on policies that currently exist at the benchmark universities.

6.1 Recognition of Voluntary Student Clubs

At the University of the Americas, no policy exists to provide voluntary student clubs with official university recognition and club privileges. One of the first steps in starting a club system involves determining guidelines for granting students groups the status of an officially recognized club that will be entitled to privileges determined by the universities as well as government laws.

A concern of the University of the Americas is that granting official status to voluntary student groups would be against its philosophy of being nonpartisan and nonsectarian. Many universities share this same concern and therefore have official statements to clarify the university's position. Princeton University (2000) provides a clear example:

> Recognition by the University does not imply official endorsement of the organization's ideas or activities. Student organizations may sponsor speakers of their choice and are free to hold meetings and in other ways express their views, subject only to the protection of people and property and adherence to reasonable regulations respecting time and place.

In order for a student group to secure the status of a recognized organization at Princeton, the officers of the group must complete and sign a recognition form provided by the office of the Dean of Student Life. This form requires a description of the group's purposes and activities. The form states the policies governing recognized organizations and the possible loss of status and privileges for failure to comply with these policies. Whenever officers of the student organizations change, the new officers or several members must resubmit recognition forms. In most cases, the officers must personally assume financial responsibility for the organization. As an alternative to the officers assuming financial responsibility, student organizations that are legally incorporated may provide evidence of their incorporation and a list of the governing board members.

Princeton (2000) emphasizes that it is beneficial to both the voluntary student clubs and the university for the clubs to be officially recognized and to have their activities approved. For the university, it is important to assure that the activities of the voluntary student organizations are consistent with the university's purposes. For the voluntary student clubs, officially recognized status provides the clubs with many privileges.

Yale University appears to require that all voluntary student groups be registered. According to Yale (2000):

> Any undergraduate organization that conducts meetings periodically or sponsors activities on the campus of Yale University, that provides a service, or that raises funds within the University for charitable or other purposes must register annually with the Office of Student Affairs of the Yale College Dean's Office.

Regardless whether registration of voluntary student clubs is encouraged or required, Princeton, Yale, and the other benchmark universities have established registration procedures for clubs to apply for official recognition. These procedures facilitate the application process and provide guidelines for both the university and the voluntary student clubs.

6.2 Criteria for Voluntary Student Clubs

In order to determine if a group will be granted official recognition, criteria must be established for voluntary student clubs. Stanford University (2000, Sept.) states:

> voluntary student organizations are groups or clubs formed for a specific task or purpose. Their structure may be either formal or informal. Some local groups are affiliated with national organizations, but the local campus organization and its student membership must make all Stanford decisions.

Stanford (2000, Sept.) requires voluntary student organizations to meet the following criteria:

- Membership is not mandatory.
- Membership is both open and limited to current Stanford students.
- Other members of the Stanford community (faculty, staff, and alumni) may participate in organizational activities, but they cannot be considered organization members.
- Stanford students must make all organizational decisions and hold all leadership positions (including that of Authorized Representative).
- Members of the Stanford community other than current students may serve in an advisory role but cannot lead or direct the organization's activities in any way.
- New groups must not duplicate the goals and activities of existing student organizations.

Other universities may have additional criteria for deciding whether to grant official recognition to a group. Usually, universities must consider such factors as the federal, state and local laws for granting or denying recognition to a particular group. The denial of recognition by the university to a group based on such factors as race or religion could be regarded as discrimination.

In the case of the University of the Americas, the school must consider a number of factors. While the university is located in Mexico and subject to Mexican laws, it is also accredited in the United States through the Southern Association of Colleges and Schools. Therefore, the university must take into account not only Mexican laws and requirements, but must also follow the rules and regulations of the Southern Association of Colleges and Schools. The University of the Americas may also need to consider additional factors in drafting a policy since it is associated with many organizations and universities in the U.S. and throughout the world.

After establishing the criteria for voluntary student clubs, the university must respond to groups seeking recognition. MIT (2001) divides its decisions for official recognition into three categories:

- The group will be provisionally recognized if there are no technical problems with the group's constitution, no questions about the group having a distinct purpose, and the statement indicates that the founders have a clear plan of action for their group.
- The group will not be recognized. This result may be for a variety of reasons including: the group's purpose is already being served by another campus organization or that recognition is not appropriate for the group. A group not receiving recognition can appeal this decision by meeting with the Association of Student Activities Executive Board.

- Revisions to the application are requested. If there are technical problems with the application, like missing clauses in the constitution, the group will be provided with instructions on what is wrong and how to correct it. If there are more subtle or complicated problems with the constitution, the Association of Student Activities Executive Board may request a meeting with the group's founders to discuss the application.

6.3 Privileges of Voluntary Student Clubs

An important part of a voluntary student club system involves the privileges that the officially recognized clubs are granted. Policy must be drafted that define these privileges as well as reasons for the loss them. Since the University of the Americas currently has no established policy for voluntary student clubs, students have no viable means of securing any privileges.

All of the benchmark universities provide a list of the privileges granted to recognized student organizations. Although the lists may vary from one university to another, the general content is usually similar. The basic privileges usually include:

- The use university facilities
- The use of the university name
- Permission to post advertisements of events on campus
- Permission to fundraise
- University funding
- Club websites

6.4 Christian Religious Clubs

According Harvard University (1998), religion can be an important part of the educational experience that can involve:

- Freedom to explore belief and life choices
- Deeper engagement of your own faith tradition
- Exploration of other faiths
- Support and renewal in community worship
- Discovery and growth through the study of the scriptures
- Integration of faith commitments and academic work
- Grounding in individual and social ethics
- Challenges to justice and bias
- Opportunities for ministry in volunteer service

As mentioned in the introduction, the University of the Americas maintains a strict policy that prohibits religious activity or expression on campus. This policy would effectually prohibit Christian religious clubs. This thesis has demonstrated that this type of policy is inconsistent with the benchmark universities that allow Christian religious clubs as well as other non-Christian religious clubs. The reason the University of the Americas maintains this policy is based on the University's philosophy of being independent from any religious affiliation. The University's concern could be addressed by the drafting of a statement similar to ones used by the benchmark universities, which states that recognition of a club does not imply endorsement of the club by the university. Since Christian religious clubs are some of the most common student clubs, the University of the Americas may need to reevaluate their policy regarding religion if it decides to begin a voluntary student club system.

By prohibiting Christian religious clubs, the University of the Americas and the students suffer a great loss. Christian religious clubs contribute to student life and the overall educational experience. In addition to the benefits identified in this thesis for voluntary student clubs, Christian religious clubs can help to provide the university community with a better understanding and greater appreciation of:

- The Bible
- The influence of Christianity in art, music, and literature
- The influence of Christianity on law and the legal system
- The influence of Christianity on education
- The contributions of Christianity to science
- Denominations and religious practices within Christianity
- Western Civilization
- Judaism
- Islam
- Ancient and Modern Middle Eastern civilizations

While the University of the Americas places a strong emphasis on international relations, most of their students know little about an important topic in international relations – religion. Even when focusing on western civilization, most students at the University's have limited knowledge about the many different denominations within Christianity. To have a well-rounded education, students at the University of the Americas need to learn more about religion and the religious practices of others. It is important for the students to learn to speak intelligently with people of other religions without arguing, getting angry, or becoming notably quiet. A voluntary student club system that included religious clubs could provide the opportunity for students to develop their knowledge, understanding, appreciation, and respect of other religions.

In addition to academic and cultural contributions, Christian religious clubs can help provide comfort, encouragement and spiritual guidance. Students attending college often have spiritual needs and concerns. Officially recognized Christian religious clubs can help to provide students with support in this area.

6.5 Religious Student Clubs and the Mexican Constitution

While Mexico is strongly Catholic, at the same time the country is politically secular. In regard to education, most Mexicans, including students, administration and faculty at the University of the Americas, have been influenced by early versions of the Mexican constitution that stressed the separation of church and state (Brock and Clarkson 1990). Concerning education, the original Mexican constitution of 1917 states:

> I. Freedom of religious beliefs being guaranteed by Article 24, the standard which shall guide such education shall be maintained entirely apart from any religious doctrine and, based on the results of scientific progress, shall strive against ignorance and its effects, servitudes, fanaticism, and prejudice….
>
> IV. Religious corporations, ministers of religion, stock companies which exclusively or predominantly engage in educational activities, and associations or companies devoted to propagation of any religious creed shall not in any way participate in institutions giving elementary, secondary and normal education and education for laborers or field workers (Pan American Union 1968).

The original Mexican constitution has been amended throughout the years. In 1933, the bias against religion intensified and the constitution was expanded to make education more secular and socialist (Brock and Clarkson 1990). In 1996, however, a greater tolerance toward religion led to an amending of the constitution that provided effectual religious freedom in the field of education. The constitution now states:

> I. As Article 24 guarantees freedom of beliefs, education will be independent of church beliefs and as such, it will be completely free of any religious doctrine.
>
> II. This education will be based on the results of scientific progress and will aid the student in struggling against ignorance and its effects--slavery, fanaticism, and prejudice.
>
> V. Besides providing preschool, primary, and secondary education, the State will promote and assist in all types and means of education, including higher education

necessary for the development of the Nation. Education will support scientific and technological research, and advance the strengthening and spread of our culture.

VII. Universities and other institutions of higher education to which the law grants autonomy, will have the power, ability, and responsibility to govern themselves, achieve their ends of education, research, and spreading culture in agreement with the principles of this article, respecting freedom of teaching and research and of free examination and discussion of ideas, will determine their plans and programs, fix the terms of salary, promotion, and tenure of their academic personnel, and administer their own property. Labor relations, of academic as well as administrative personnel, will be conducted according to part A of Article 123 of this Constitution, in the terms and with the means that the Federal Labor Law establishes in conformance with the characteristics of special work, in a manner that agrees with autonomy, freedom of teaching, and research, and the ends of the institutions to which this section refers… (Pamachena 2001, Dec.).

The new language stating that education will be "independent of church beliefs" rather than "maintained entirely apart from any religious doctrine" emphasizes a separation from church, but not specifically from theology or religious philosophy. The former wording gave the impression that "ignorance" was religious beliefs. The new wording, however, stating that education "will aid the student in struggling against ignorance" appears to refer to ignorance as the lack of knowledge. The original restrictions of clause IV have been eliminated which had forbidden participation in education by: "Religious corporations, ministers of religion,…and associations or companies devoted to propagation of any religious creed." The new phrase: "the State will promote and assist in all types and means of education" appears include religious education.

The new language in general appears to encourage diversity and freedom of expression. The amended constitution declares that autonomous universities "respecting freedom of teaching and research and of free examination and discussion of ideas, will determine their plans and programs, … and administer their own property." Furthermore, labor relations are to be conducted "in a manner that agrees with . . . freedom of teaching, and research…"

In view of these important changes to the constitution, if the University of the Americas began a voluntary student club system, it apparently should be able to include religious clubs. The amended Mexican constitution appears to support religious clubs, whereas previously religious clubs may have been a violation of the law.

As demonstrated in this thesis, all of the benchmark universities grant official recognition to religious voluntary student clubs and extend to them full privileges. While Jewish, Islamic, and other non-Christian religious clubs often exist on campus, Christian religious clubs are usually the most common. If the University of the Americas decides to initiate a voluntary student club system, it should consider allowing Christian religious clubs as well as other non-Christian religious clubs.

Epilogue

The thesis was well received by the University of the Americas, but not all of the recommendations were followed. The University now has a policy for clubs, however, the policy discriminates against religious and political clubs. This thesis described the benefits of religious clubs, particularly Christian religious clubs. Although Jewish, Islamic, and other non-Christian religious clubs often exist on campus, Christian religious clubs are normally the most common. This University of the Americas's policy is different from all of the benchmark universities which grant official recognition and extend full privileges to religious voluntary student clubs.

The University now has a web page with information on voluntary student clubs. The web page lists 18 student organizations, many, or perhaps all, appear meet the criteria of a voluntary student club. The page also includes an application form to begin a club. Below is a translation of part of the web page of the University of the Americas (2011):

> To be part of an Organization offers the possibility of developing diverse abilities and creating a social conscience. On the campus, organizations exist created and directed by students.
>
> The organizations are work teams formed by students who identify themselves by a similar interest, share a common objective, and offer to the student community places for participation to share this objective and complete activities that enrich their experience and those that interact with them. They formulate a plan and develop their projects.
>
> It is possible to be an active member and to integrate yourself to a work team of some Organization; you simply need to contact the Organization and request entrance. You can be an affiliate member and request that they send you information via email, and you will be able to be part of the activities and not necessarily the work team.
>
> Being part of a Student Organization is an opportunity to put restlessness into action and to be an agent of change, to put into practice and to develop different abilities, to acquire experience that can have important professional value for many companies and to meet people, to make friends, etc.
>
> All Organizations must be formed by students of the University of the Americas Puebla and the objective of the Organization must be in accordance with the mission, philosophy and values of the University. It needs to have clear purpose, and an

Organization with the same objective must not exist, the purpose of the Organization must be neither political nor religious, a minimum five people are required to form a work team and the Organization must be open to all of the student community.

Dr. Nora Lustig, rector from 2001-2005, initiated change that opened the doors for voluntary student clubs at the University of the Americas. Hopefully, in the future, the University of the Americas will revise their policy to allow Christian religious clubs as well as other religious clubs.

Bibliography

Astin, Alexander W. (1985) "Involvement: The Cornerstone of Excellence" Change. July/August: pp 35-39

- - - (1984, July) "Student Involvement: A Developmental Theory for Higher Education" Journal of College Student Personnel. pp. 297-307

Balian, Edward S. (1988) How To Design, Analyze, And Write Doctoral Or Maters Research. Laham, MD: University Press of America,

Ball, Don and McCulloch, Wendell. (1999) International Business. Boston, MA: McGraw-Hill, pp 9-12.

Besson, Taunee. (1994) The Wall Street Journal National Business Employment Weekly Resumes. New York: John Wiley & Sons, Inc. pp. 72-73

Bogan, Christopher E.; and English, Michael J. (1994) Benchmarking For Best Practices: Winning Through Innovative Adaptation. New York: McGraw-Hill, p. 1-3

Botzman, Thomas J. and Kim, Hyun Sook Lee. (1997) "International Higher Education System Teaching International Business in the Era of Free Trade" Dec. 2001, http://www.muc.edu/~botzmatj/teach.html

Boyer, Ernest L. (1990) Campus Life: In Search of Community. Princeton, NJ: The Carnegie Foundation for the Advancement of Teaching, pp. 48-49

- - - (1987) College: The Undergraduate Experience In America. New York: Harper & Row Publishers, pp. 191-218

Brock, Colin and Clarkson, Donald (1990) Education in Central America and the Caribbean. New York: Chapman and Hall, Inc.

Brubaker, John S. and Rudy, Willis. (1976) Higher Education in Transition: A history of American colleges and universities, 1636-1976. New York: Harper and Row Publishers, pp. 131-132

California Institute of Technology (2000, Nov.) "Beyond Studying" Pasadena, CA, http://www.admissions.caltech.edu/beyond/clubs.htm

Carnegie, Dale and Associates, Inc. (1993) The Leader In You: How to Win Friends, Influence People, and Succeed in a Changing World. New York: Simon & Schuster, pp. 19-29

Chesla, Erik (2000) Successful Teamwork: How To Become A Team Player. New York: Learning Express, pp. 3-19

Colby, Kimberlee W. (1993) Center for Law and Religious Freedom, Annandale, Virginia, Aug. 2000, http://www.nlrc.org/public/docs/guide.htm

Collier, D.A. (1994) The Service Quality Solution: Using Service Management to Gain Competitive Advantage. Milwaukee, WI: Irwin,

Currie, Jan and Newson, Janice. (1998) Universities and Globalization: Critical Perspectives. Thousand Oaks, CA: SAGE Publications, Inc.

Delta Upsilon (2002, Feb.) "The History of Delta Upsilon" http://www.deltau.org

DeVellis, Robert F. (1991) Scale Development: Theory and Applications. Newbury Park, CA: Sage Publications, Inc., pp. 12-13 and 83.

Emory, C. William (1985) Business Research Methods. Homewood, IL: Richard D. Irwin, Inc., pp. 27-28, 260--281

"Entrepreneur" (2000, Dec.) Merriam-Webster Online Collegiate Dictionary. http://www.m-w.com/dictionary.htm

Eppers, Rhonda Martin (1999) "Applying Benchmarking to Higher Education" Change November/December pp.24-31

Fry, Ron (1996) Your First Resume 4th ed. Franklin Lakes, NJ: Career Press, pp. 98

Grönroos, C. (1990) "Managing the Service Product: The Augmented Service Offering" In Service Management and Marketing: Managing Moments of Truth in Service Competition. Lexington, KY: Lexington Books, pp. 71-91

Harvard, (2000) Student Handbook Cambridge, MA: Harvard, http://www.registrar.fas.harvard.edu/handbooks/student/chapter8/index.html

- - - (1998, Nov.) Cambridge, MA: Harvard, http://www.harvard.edu

Horowitz, Helen Lefkowitz (1987) <u>Campus Life: Undergraduate Cultures from the End of the Eighteenth Century to the Present</u>. Chicago: The University of Chicago Press, pp. 13, 23, 28-29, 41, 54-55, 61 and 108-119

Instituto Tecnológico Autónomo de México, (2001, Oct.) México, México, http://www.itam.mx

Kelley, Scott W., Donnelly James H., and Skinner, Steven J. (1990) "Customer Participation in Service Production and Delivery" <u>Journal of Retailing</u>, Vol. 66, No. 3 (Fall), pp. 315-335

Kent, Rollin (1998, Feb.) "Institutional Reform in Mexican Higher Education: Conflict and Renewal in Three Public Universities" Washington, D.C.– No. EDU-102, December 15, 2001, http://www.iadb.org/sds/doc/edu%2D102e.pdf

Levine, Arthur (1980) <u>When Dreams and Heroes Died: A Portrait of Today's College Student</u>. San Francisco: The Carnegie Foundation for the Advancement of Teaching, Jossey-Bass Publishers, Inc., pp. 94-101

Levine, Arthur and Cureton, Jeanette S. (1998) <u>When Hope and Fear Collide: A Portrait of Today's College Student</u>. San Francisco: Jossey-Bass Publishers, Inc., pp. 55-63

Macionis, John J. (1991) <u>Sociology</u> 3rd ed. Englewood Cliffs, NJ: Prentice Hall, pp. 119-145

MIT Association of Student Activities (2001, April) "How to Start a Student Activity" Cambridge, MA http://web.mit.edu/asa/www/new-activity.html

MIT Student Advisory Committee (1998, April) <u>Putting Education First</u> Cambridge, MA: MIT http://web.mit.edu/ committees/sll/final.html

MIT Presidential Task Force on Student Life and Learning (1998, Sept.) Cambridge MA: MIT http://web.mit.edu/evolving/student.html

Morison, Samuel Eliot (1964) <u>Three Centuries of Harvard</u>. Cambridge, MA: The Belknap Press of Harvard University, pp. 61-62

Oblinger, Diana G. and Verville, Anne-Lee (1998) <u>What Business Wants From Higher Education</u>. Phoenix, AZ.: American Council on Education, Oryx Press, pp. 21-23

Pascarcella, Ernest T. and Terenzini, Patrick T. (1991) How College Affects Students. San Francisco: Jossey-Bass Publishers, p. 624

Pan American Union, General Secretariat, Organization of American States, (1968) "1917 Constitution of Mexico" Washington, D.C., Text translated from *Constitución Política de los Estados Unidos Mexicanos*, Trigésima Quinta Edición, 1967, Editorial Porrua, S. A., México, D. F. December 15, 2001, http://www.ilstu.edu/class/hist263/docs/1917const.html

Pamachena, Ron. (2001, Dec.) "Mexican Constitution as of 1996" Hereford, AZ: Sycamore Research Services, http://historicaltextarchive.com/mexico/constitution.html

Porter, Michael E. (1985) Competitive Advantage: Creating and Sustaining Superior Performance. New York: The Free Press, pp. xvi, 33-34

- - - (1990) The Competitive Advantage of the Nations. New York: The Free Press, pp. 40-43

Princeton (1999) Rights, Rules, Responsibilities Princeton, NJ: Princeton, http://www.princeton.edu/pr/pub/rrr/99/pages/41.htm

- - - (2000) The Princeton University Student Organization Sourcebook. Princeton, NJ: Princeton, http://webware.princeton.edu/stulife/stuorgs/sorgman.htm#Stand_Up_and_ Be_Recognized

Reisberg, Leo (2000, Sept.) "Proliferation of campus clubs: Too much of a good thing?" Chronicle of Higher Education. pp. 47-48.

Rosen, Robert H. (1996) Leading People. New York: Penguin Group, pp. 3-23

Rudolf, Fredrick (1977) Curriculum: A History of the American Undergraduate Course of Study Since 1636. San Francisco: Jossey-Bass Publishers, pp.14, 94-98

- - - (1962) The American College And University. New York: Alfred A. Knopf, pp.145-146

Sasser, W. E. (1984) "Mach Supply and Demand in Service Industries" In Service Marketing: Text, Cases & Readings under the Direction of Christopher H. Lovelock, pp. 330-338. Englewood Cliffs, NJ: Prentice Hall

Shefsky, Lloyd E. (1994) Entrepreneurs Are Made Not Born. New York: McGraw-Hill, Inc., pp. 1-22

Shostack, G.L. (1984) "Breaking Free from Product Marketing" In <u>Service Marketing: Text, Cases & Readings</u>. Under the direction of Lovelock, C.H, Englewood Cliffs, NJ, Prentice Hall, pp.37-47

Spendolini, Michael J. (1992) <u>The Benchmarking Book</u>. New York: American Management Association, p. 3-9

Stanford (2000, Sept) <u>Student Organization Handbook</u>. Stanford, CA: Office of Student Activities, http://www.stanford.edu/dept/OSA/Resources/soh/soh.html

- - - (2000, Sept) "Student Affairs Core Values" Stanford, CA http://www.stanford.edu/dept/ vpsa/ contactingstanford/Vision_Mission%20Statement.htm

Stage, Frances K. (1992) <u>Diverse Methods for Research and Assessment of College Students</u>. Alexandria, VA: American College Personnel Association, pp. 15

Tecnológico de Monterrey, (2001, Oct.) Monterrey, México, http://www.mty.itesm.mx

Tucker, Ruth A. (1983) <u>From Jerusalem to Irianjaya: A Biographical History of Christian Missions</u>. Grand Rapids, Michigan: The Zondervan Corporation, pp. 122-476

Universidad Anahuac (2001, Oct.) México, México, http://www.uas.mx/

Universidad Autónoma de Guadalajara (2001, Oct.) Guadalajara, Jalisco, México http://www.gdl.uag.mx/

Universidad De La Salle (2001, Oct.) México, México, www.delasalle.edu.mx

Universidad de las Américas (2001, Dec.) San Andrés Cholula, Puebla
http://www.udlap.mx/pg2/pres/historia.html
http://www.udlap.mx/pg2/pres/sintesis.html

Universidad de las Américas (2011, May.) San Andrés Cholula, Puebla
http://www.udlap.mx/vidaEstudiantil/asociaciones.aspx

Universidad Iberoamericana Santa Fe (2001, Oct.) México, México, http://www.uia.mx

University of Pennsylvania (1997) "Activities and Organizations" Philadelphia, PA: The Practical Penn, University of Pennsylvania, http://dolphin.upenn.edu/~pracpenn/pp13a_orgs.html

- - - (1999, January) "University Life Facilities, Technology, and Information Services" Philadelphia, PA: University of Pennsylvania, http://pobox.upenn.edu/ %7Etech/

- - - (2000, Aug.) "Mission of the University Life Division" Philadelphia, PA: University of Pennsylvania http://www.upenn.edu/osl/vprovost.html

Upcraft, M. Lee (1985) "Residence Halls and Campus Activities" In <u>Increasing Student Retention</u>. Noel, Lee, Levitz, Randi, Saluri, Diana and Associates, Jossey-Bass Publishers, pp. 330-333

- - - (1990) "Residence Halls and Campus Activities" In <u>The Freshman Year Experience</u>. Upcraft, M. Lee, Gardner, John N. and Associates, San Francisco: Jossey-Bass Publishers, pp. 142-155

US News Online (2000, Aug.) "2001 College Rankings" http://www.usnews.com/usnews/edu/college/rankings/natunivs/natu_a2.htm

Weingartener, Rudolph H. (1993) <u>Undergraduate Education Goals and Means</u>. Phoenix, AZ: American Council on Education, Oryx Press, pp. 119-123

Yale (2000, Sept.) New Haven, CT: The Office of the Dean of Student Affairs, http://www.yale.edu/studentaffairs/

- - - (2002, Jan.) New Haven, CT, Yale http://www.yale.edu/chaplain/programs/index.html

Appendix A
Sample Questionnaire

Dear

     I am working on my master's thesis and would very much appreciate if you could take a minute to answer a brief survey. The survey below is directed to university faculty and staff, and alumni administrators regarding their opinions on voluntary student clubs. These clubs would not include student government, fraternities or sport teams. To respond, simply include the original message and answer the questions. Thank you very much.

Sincerely,
James Daughtry
MBA Student
University of the Americas

Please put an X above the space that most accurately reflects your opinion on each question. If you are unable to provide an opinion, put an X above the space NR (No Response).

1. What effect does participation in voluntary student clubs have on:

Social development of students?
(Negative)   (Positive)
__ __ __ __ __ __ __   NR __

Developing leadership ability?
(Negative)   (Positive)
__ __ __ __ __ __ __   NR __

Building of self-esteem?
(Negative)   (Positive)
__ __ __ __ __ __ __   NR __

Instilling an entrepreneur spirit?
(Negative)   (Positive)
__ __ __ __ __ __ __   NR __

Assuming responsibility?
(Negative)   (Positive)
— — — — — — —   NR __

Encouraging teamwork?
(Negative)   (Positive)
— — — — — — —   NR __

Academic performance?
(Negative)   (Positive)
— — — — — — —   NR __

Promoting ethical values?
(Negative)   (Positive)
— — — — — — —   NR __

Alumni giving?
(Negative)   (Positive)
— — — — — — —   NR __

The hiring decisions of companies?
(Negative)   (Positive)
— — — — — — —   NR __

2. What effect do voluntary student clubs have on:

Attracting students to the university?
(Negative)   (Positive)
— — — — — — —   NR __

The retention rate of students?
(Negative)   (Positive)
— — — — — — —   NR __

Adding value to the university?
(Negative)   (Positive)
— — — — — — —   NR __

The overall college experience?
(Negative)　　　　(Positive)

__ __ __ __ __ __ __　　NR __

Name of University (where you are employed):

Department:

Area of Specialty:

How many years do you have working at this university?

How many years have you worked in the education field?

Please put an X above the space for your age group:

__ 20-29 __ 30-39 __ 40-49 __ 50 and over

Please put an X above the space for your gender:

__ Male　　__ Female

If you have any comments, please provide them below.
Thank you for your time and assistance. Comments:

Appendix B
Pilot Test Questionnaire Data

Survey	1a	1b	1c	1d	1e	1f	1g	1h	1i	1j	2a	2b	2c	2d
1	7	7	7	5	5	7	9	9	7	9	7	7	7	7
2	7	7	7	4	7	7	4	7	9	6	9	5	9	7
3	6	4	6	3	5	5	6	3	2	4	4	5	5	6
4	7	7	7	7	7	7	7	7	7	7	7	7	7	7
5	4	5	5	4	5	5	4	4	4	6	9	4	5	6
6	6	7	6	4	4	6	6	9	9	6	5	7	6	6
7	7	7	5	9	6	5	4	5	4	7	6	5	7	7
8	6	5	6	4	6	7	5	9	4	5	5	5	6	7
9	6	7	7	5	6	5	7	4	5	4	5	4	6	7
10	7	7	7	7	7	7	4	7	7	7	4	5	7	7
11	7	7	6	4	4	6	4	6	9	5	7	7	7	5
12	6	6	5	4	5	5	5	5	4	6	5	4	5	6
13	7	6	6	5	6	6	5	5	9	9	6	5	6	6
14	7	7	7	5	6	7	4	6	7	7	5	7	7	7
15	7	6	5	4	6	7	5	6	6	6	7	6	6	6
16	6	6	6	4	6	6	4	6	4	6	9	9	6	7
17	6	7	6	7	6	5	3	3	7	7	7	6	5	6
18	5	5	5	5	5	5	4	4	9	5	6	5	6	6
19	6	5	7	9	5	6	4	9	9	5	6	5	7	6
20	6	4	5	9	4	6	4	6	9	6	9	9	6	6
21	6	5	6	4	7	6	5	4	6	5	6	7	6	6
22	6	5	5	6	4	5	4	4	9	9	5	4	6	7
23	6	6	5	6	6	7	4	5	4	5	5	6	6	6
24	7	6	5	6	6	7	5	5	9	9	6	6	6	7
25	7	7	7	6	7	7	5	6	7	7	6	6	7	7
26	7	7	7	7	7	7	7	7	7	7	7	7	7	7
27	6	6	4	5	5	5	4	4	4	5	5	4	6	6
28	6	6	5	6	6	6	5	9	4	9	7	5	6	6
29	7	7	7	7	7	7	5	7	9	7	7	7	7	7
30	6	5	5	4	6	6	9	4	9	5	5	9	5	7

Prepared by author using the pilot test raw data and the semantic space values in section 3.6.

Appendix C
Reliability Analysis – Scale (Alpha)

SPSS 6.1 for the Power Macintosh
Method 2 (covariance matrix) was used for this analysis

Correlation Matrix

	A1	A10	A2	A3	A4
A1	1.0000				
A10	.4282	1.0000			
A2	.5891	.6349	1.0000		
A3	.5365	.3897	.5313	1.0000	
A4	.4688	.6243	.7959	.4681	1.0000
A5	.6418	.4933	.5511	.7154	.6381
A6	.7195	.5451	.4580	.4459	.4762
A7	.2981	-.2064	.0712	.4465	.0488
A8	.6650	.6522	.5716	.4567	.4657
A9	.6220	.7688	.7780	.6102	.7237

	A5	A6	A7	A8	A9
A5	1.0000				
A6	.7381	1.0000			
A7	.2841	.1200	1.0000		
A8	.6268	.8378	.2432	1.0000	
A9	.7966	.6167	.0477	.5636	1.0000

N of Cases = 15.0

Item-total Statistics

	Scale Mean If Item Deleted	Scale Variance If Item Deleted	Corrected Item-Total Correlation	Squared Multiple Correlation	Alpha If Item Deleted
A1	50.9333	60.9238	.7362	.6673	.8878
A10	51.2667	58.4952	.6561	.9037	.8889
A2	51.0000	58.8571	.7618	.8951	.8842
A3	51.2000	59.3143	.6770	.7018	.8882
A4	52.0000	54.7143	.6962	.8177	.8865
A5	51.1333	59.8381	.8307	.9054	.8835
A6	51.1333	58.9810	.7341	.8740	.8854
A7	52.2667	65.6381	.1672	.6490	.9219
A8	52.0667	53.4952	.7415	.9223	.8831
A9	51.8000	49.1714	.8217	.9387	.8779

Reliability Coefficients   10 items

Alpha = .8993   Standardized item alpha = .9127

<u>Correlation Matrix</u>

	B1	B2	B3	B4
B1	1.0000			
B2	.5232	1.0000		
B3	.3188	.4571	1.0000	
B4	-.0898	.0335	.4130	1.0000

N of Cases = 25.0

Item-total Statistics

	Scale Mean If Item Deleted	Scale Variance If Item Deleted	Corrected Item-Total Correlation	Squared Multiple Correlation	Alpha If Item Deleted
B1	18.4000	3.0833	.4233	.3089	.5141
B2	18.5600	2.4233	.5433	.3725	.4023
B3	17.9600	3.6233	.5577	.3882	.4485
B4	17.8000	4.9167	.1031	.2313	.6885

Reliability Coefficients   4 items

Alpha = .6091   Standardized item alpha = .6039

Correlation Matrix

	B1	B2	B3	B4	A1
B1	1.0000				
B2	.5950	1.0000			
B3	.1643	.4944	1.0000		
B4	.0441	.2508	.8178	1.0000	
A1	.3307	.5225	.8178	.6905	1.0000
A10	.4768	.5160	.5394	.4681	.7386
A2	.3562	.1660	.5916	.7042	.5347
A3	.0992	.4285	.5864	.8571	.5476
A4	.3712	.3324	.5427	.5434	.4276
A5	.4429	.6705	.7400	.6172	.6172
A6	.2839	.6867	.8111	.5006	.8260
A7	.1906	.0698	.2243	.4304	.1871
A8	.2423	.4151	.8317	.6670	.8865
A9	.5856	.6140	.6751	.6102	.7069

	A10	A2	A3	A4	A5
A10	1.0000				
A2	.6895	1.0000			
A3	.4109	.4825	1.0000		
A4	.6773	.7905	.4410	1.0000	
A5	.5394	.4817	.6866	.6178	1.0000
A6	.5797	.3907	.3942	.4402	.7057
A7	-.2085	-.0205	.4210	-.0630	.2243
A8	.6788	.5642	.4306	.5023	.6183
A9	.8291	.7703	.5990	.6849	.8005

	A6	A7	A8	A9
A6	1.0000			
A7	.0541	1.0000		
A8	.8477	.2521	1.0000	
A9	.5985	-.0614	.6095	1.0000

N of Cases = 13.0

Item-total Statistics

	Scale Mean If Item Deleted	Scale Variance If Item Deleted	Corrected Item-Total Correlation	Squared Multiple Correlation	Alpha If Item Deleted
B1	76.6154	103.923	.4673	.	.9151
B2	76.5385	100.1026	.6070	.	.9102
B3	76.0769	102.0769	.8123	.	.9055
B4	75.7692	107.5256	.7494	.	.9108
A1	75.7692	106.6923	.8301	.	.9094
A10	76.3077	97.0641	.7429	.	.9049
A2	75.9231	101.7436	.6916	.	.9076
A3	76.1538	101.3077	.6450	.	.9088
A4	76.8462	95.9744	.6611	.	.9087
A5	76.0769	101.7436	.8342	.	.9049
A6	76.0769	100.2436	.7407	.	.9058
A7	77.1538	110.4744	.1312	.	.9298

A8	77.0769	92.0769	.7707	.	.9038
A9	76.6154	86.7564	.8519	.	.9005

Reliability Coefficients   14 items

Alpha = .9152   Standardized item alpha = .9335

Appendix D
Pilot Test Weighted Data

Survey	1a	1b	1c	1d	1e	1f	1g	1h	1i	1j	2a	2b	2c	2d
1	3	3	3	1	1	3	x	x	3	x	3	3	3	3
2	3	3	3	0	3	3	0	3	x	2	x	1	x	3
3	2	0	2	-1	1	1	2	-1	-2	0	0	1	1	2
4	3	3	3	3	3	3	3	3	3	3	3	3	3	3
5	0	1	1	0	1	1	0	0	0	2	x	0	1	2
6	2	3	2	0	0	2	2	x	x	2	1	3	2	2
7	3	3	1	x	2	1	0	1	0	3	2	1	3	3
8	2	1	2	0	2	3	1	x	0	1	1	1	2	3
9	2	3	3	1	2	1	3	0	1	0	1	0	2	3
10	3	3	3	3	3	3	0	3	3	3	0	1	3	3
11	3	3	2	0	0	2	0	2	x	1	3	3	3	1
12	2	2	1	0	1	1	1	1	0	2	1	0	1	2
13	3	2	2	1	2	2	1	1	x	x	2	1	2	2
14	3	3	3	1	2	3	0	2	3	3	1	3	3	3
15	3	2	1	0	2	3	1	2	2	2	3	2	2	2
16	2	2	2	0	2	2	0	2	0	2	x	x	2	3
17	2	3	2	3	2	1	-1	-1	3	3	3	2	1	2
18	1	1	1	1	1	1	0	0	x	1	2	1	2	2
19	2	1	3	x	1	2	0	x	x	1	2	1	3	2
20	2	0	1	x	0	2	0	2	x	2	x	x	2	2
21	2	1	2	0	3	2	1	0	2	1	2	3	2	2
22	2	1	1	2	0	1	0	0	x	x	1	0	2	3
23	2	2	1	2	2	3	0	1	0	1	1	2	2	2
24	3	2	1	2	2	3	1	1	x	x	2	2	2	3
25	3	3	3	2	3	3	1	2	3	3	2	2	3	3
26	3	3	3	3	3	3	3	3	3	3	3	3	3	3
27	2	2	0	1	1	1	0	0	0	1	1	0	2	2
28	2	2	1	2	2	2	1	x	0	x	3	1	2	2
29	3	3	3	3	3	3	1	3	x	3	3	3	3	3
30	2	1	1	0	2	2	x	0	x	1	1	x	1	3

Prepared by author using the pilot test raw data and the semantic space values in section 4.1.

Appendix E
Official Test Participant Data

Survey	Years at University	Years In Ed. Field	Age 20-29	Age 30-39	Age 40-49	Age 50+	Male	Female
1	32	32				1		1
2	2	16			1			1
3	5	18			1		1	
4	2	9		1			1	
5	4	11		1				1
6	17	30				1		1
7	13	29				1	1	
8	40	40				1		1
9	28	30				1		1
10	23	23				1		1
11	1	2		1				1
12	2.5	2.5		1				1
13	6	15			1		1	
14	3	17				1	1	
15	1	1	1					1
16	1	1			1			1
17	21	21			1			1
18	2	22			1		1	
19	5	10		1			1	
20	1	9	1					1
21	13	25				1	1	
22	5	5	1					1
23	1	25				1	1	
24	2	13		1			1	
25	3	5		1				1
26	17	21			1			1
27	22	22			1		1	
28	14	14				1		1
29	11	22			1			1
30	30	30				1		1
31	3.7	31				1	1	
32	12	12				1		1
33	26	26				1	1	
34	25	25				1		1
35	11	11			1			1
36	22	33				1	1	
37	1	1	1					1
38	1	20			1			1
39	17	17			1			1
40	12	12			1			1
41	15	15			1		1	
42	4	15			1			1
43	2	7		1				1
44	16	16			1		1	
45	21	21			1			1

Survey	Years at University	Years In Ed. Field	Age 20-29	Age 30-39	Age 40-49	Age 50+	Male	Female
46	1	3	1					1
47	6	27				1	1	
48	6	20			1		1	
49	14	25				1	1	
50	20	20				1		1
51	28	28				1		1
52	2	8		1				1
53	2	4	1				1	
54	20	29				1		1
55	22	30				1		1
56	2	2	1					1
57	7	8	1					1
58	24	27			1			1
59	1	5		1				1
60	7	12		1				1
61	13	16			1			1
62	3	10		1				1
63	10	12		1				1
64	8	18				1		1
65	1	1	1				1	
66	19	19			1		1	
67	2	7		1				1
68	4	4		1			1	
69	30	35				1		1
70	1	2.5		1				1
71	5	12		1				1
72	5	8		1				1
73	29	33				1	1	
74	1	1		1			1	
75	4	13			1			1
76	1	3	1					1
77	12	12			1			1
78	21	27				1	1	
79	20	22				1	1	
80	15	19				1	1	
81	18	18			1			1
82	1	1	1					1
83	2	4		1			1	
84	7	7		1				1
85	1	1	1					1
86	17	28				1	1	
87	17	17				1	1	
88	9	13		1			1	
89	6	6	1				1	
90	5	5			1			1
91	8	16				1		1

Prepared by author using the official test raw data.

Appendix F
Official Test Weighted Data

Survey	1a	1b	1c	1d	1e	1f	1g	1h	1i	1j	2a	2b	2c	2d
1	3	3	3	3	3	3	1	1	1	1	1	0	3	3
2	1	1	1	0	0	1	0	-1	x	x	0	x	1	2
3	2	2	1	2	1	1	0	-1	0	-1	-1	-2	1	1
4	2	2	1	0	2	3	0	1	1	0	2	1	2	2
5	0	1	2	3	-1	-1	x	-1	x	3	0	x	0	1
6	2	2	2	2	2	2	2	x	x	2	2	2	2	2
7	3	3	3	x	x	3	0	x	x	x	x	x	3	3
8	2	2	2	0	3	3	0	0	0	1	1	1	1	2
9	3	3	3	3	3	3	1	3	1	x	2	3	3	3
10	2	2	x	1	0	2	-1	x	x	x	3	x	1	3
11	1	2	2	1	2	1	0	2	0	0	1	0	1	1
12	3	2	2	x	2	2	x	x	2	x	2	2	2	2
13	3	3	3	-1	3	3	0	3	x	x	3	x	3	3
14	2	3	1	2	3	1	-2	1	2	2	1	0	2	3
15	3	1	1	1	1	2	2	3	0	1	1	1	2	3
16	3	3	2	2	2	3	0	0	2	3	3	3	3	3
17	2	3	2	1	2	2	0	1	1	1	2	2	2	2
18	2	2	2	x	2	2	1	1	0	2	2	2	x	2
19	3	3	3	-1	3	3	-1	0	0	-1	0	0	3	3
20	3	2	1	0	1	1	0	0	1	1	2	2	3	2
21	3	3	3	2	3	3	0	x	2	1	2	2	3	3
22	2	0	2	x	2	2	2	2	x	x	x	x	2	2
23	2	2	2	1	2	1	0	1	x	2	0	2	2	2
24	1	1	0	2	1	2	0	0	1	0	x	x	2	2
25	3	3	3	1	3	3	1	3	2	3	1	2	3	3
26	3	3	3	1	1	3	2	1	2	2	2	2	3	3
27	2	2	1	1	2	2	1	2	x	x	0	1	2	2
28	2	2	2	2	2	2	-1	0	0	1	-1	-1	0	1
29	2	3	2	x	3	3	2	x	2	3	2	3	3	3
30	2	3	2	x	2	3	x	x	x	x	x	x	2	2
31	2	2	2	1	2	2	1	0	1	1	1	2	2	2
32	x	2	2	2	2	2	x	x	2	2	x	x	2	2
33	3	3	3	3	3	3	0	0	2	2	2	2	2	2
34	2	2	1	1	1	2	-1	0	0	2	0	x	2	3
35	3	3	3	0	2	3	-1	2	2	1	0	1	1	3
36	3	3	3	-1	3	3	-1	-1	x	x	x	-1	-1	1
37	3	2	2	0	1	2	1	2	0	2	3	3	3	3
38	3	3	3	3	x	3	3	3	3	3	3	3	3	3
39	1	2	2	2	x	0	-2	x	x	x	x	-2	1	1
40	1	1	2	1	2	0	-1	1	x	2	2	x	2	2
41	3	3	3	1	2	2	0	1	x	2	x	x	2	2
42	2	2	1	2	1	2	x	1	2	x	x	x	2	2
43	3	3	3	-1	0	1	1	0	x	x	x	x	3	3
44	1	1	0	0	1	0	0	0	1	0	0	0	1	1
45	2	0	1	0	1	0	0	0	1	1	2	2	1	2

Survey	1a	1b	1c	1d	1e	1f	1g	1h	1i	1j	2a	2b	2c	2d
46	3	3	3	3	3	3	2	2	2	3	x	x	3	3
47	3	3	3	1	3	3	2	2	1	3	3	2	3	3
48	3	3	3	1	3	3	1	2	2	2	2	3	2	2
49	1	2	1	1	1	1	-1	0	x	0	1	1	2	2
50	2	1	1	0	-1	2	0	0	2	1	-1	0	3	3
51	3	3	3	0	3	3	3	0	x	x	0	0	3	3
52	3	3	3	3	3	3	3	3	3	3	x	3	3	3
53	2	2	1	0	0	1	1	-1	1	0	0	2	2	2
54	2	2	1	1	2	0	-2	1	2	x	x	-1	3	2
55	3	3	3	3	3	3	x	x	x	3	x	3	3	3
56	3	3	3	0	3	3	3	2	2	2	3	3	3	3
57	3	3	3	2	2	2	1	1	1	0	1	1	3	3
58	3	3	3	2	3	3	1	2	1	2	3	2	3	3
59	2	2	3	1	2	2	0	0	0	1	2	2	1	1
60	3	x	3	2	3	3	1	2	0	0	2	1	3	2
61	3	3	0	0	2	2	0	0	x	2	2	1	2	3
62	2	3	1	1	2	1	0	0	1	2	1	1	1	1
63	2	1	1	1	1	2	0	0	2	1	3	0	3	2
64	2	2	2	2	3	2	0	0	1	1	1	1	2	1
65	2	2	1	1	1	1	0	0	x	2	2	1	2	3
66	3	3	3	2	2	3	1	1	x	2	3	1	3	3
67	3	1	1	-1	1	1	1	1	0	0	1	0	3	3
68	3	3	3	x	2	1	0	0	x	2	3	1	2	3
69	1	0	0	0	1	1	2	0	2	3	2	2	2	2
70	2	1	1	0	1	3	x	1	1	1	1	1	2	2
71	-1	1	-1	-1	1	1	0	2	0	2	2	1	3	2
72	2	2	2	2	2	2	-1	2	2	2	x	-1	-1	0
73	2	2	2	0	2	2	-1	1	1	1	0	-1	1	1
74	2	1	2	1	1	2	0	1	2	1	2	0	2	2
75	3	3	3	3	3	3	x	3	3	3	2	2	3	3
76	3	3	3	1	3	3	1	0	1	2	0	1	1	1
77	2	2	1	3	1	2	1	0	1	2	2	2	3	3
78	3	3	2	3	3	3	2	2	2	x	3	2	2	2
79	2	1	2	0	2	2	0	1	2	1	1	1	1	2
80	2	2	2	x	2	3	0	0	3	2	3	x	2	3
81	0	1	1	1	0	0	1	-1	1	0	-1	-1	-1	-1
82	3	3	3	3	3	3	1	3	1	3	3	3	3	3
83	3	3	3	3	3	3	0	2	3	2	3	3	3	3
84	3	3	3	2	2	1	-1	0	3	1	3	3	3	3
85	1	1	0	0	2	2	0	0	0	x	1	2	3	2
86	2	2	2	2	2	2	1	2	1	1	3	3	3	3
87	3	3	3	3	3	3	1	2	x	x	2	1	3	3
88	3	3	3	1	2	3	2	2	2	2	0	3	3	3
89	2	1	1	0	1	2	-2	2	x	0	1	2	3	3
90	1	1	1	x	1	1	1	x	1	x	1	1	1	1
91	3	3	3	x	3	3	x	2	1	1	0	0	3	3

Prepared by author using the official test raw data and the semantic scale values in section 4.1.

Notes

www.ingramcontent.com/pod-product-compliance
Lightning Source LLC
Chambersburg PA
CBHW081218230426
43666CB00015B/2790